BECOMING A MATHEMATICS SPECIALIST TEACHER

What is the role of the mathematics specialist?

What is deep subject knowledge in mathematics?

What sort of pedagogical knowledge does a mathematics specialist need?

How can you best support your colleagues to improve mathematics teaching and learning?

Becoming a Primary Mathematics Specialist Teacher helps you explore the role of the specialist in promoting positive attitudes towards mathematics and developing the teaching and learning of mathematics in your primary school.

Illustrated throughout with classroom-based examples and referenced to relevant research, it is designed to support your development as a reflective practitioner who can confidently review and develop practice in your own classroom, as well as challenge and move the whole school forward through collaborative professional development. Essential topics explored include:

- the nature of the role of the primary mathematics specialist;
- understanding how attitudes to mathematics evolve, and why it is crucial to challenge and change negativity;
- what we mean by deep subject knowledge in primary mathematics;
- pedagogical knowledge of how mathematics is taught and learned;
- the skills of coaching and mentoring to support teachers and teaching assistants;
- unpicking the principles of progression for high-quality teaching in all year groups;
- the key features of deep subject knowledge and pedagogy in three areas of the curriculum: multiplication, time and data handling.

Becoming a Primary Mathematics Specialist Teacher is an essential source of guidance and ideas for all primary school teachers aiming to achieve Mathematics Specialist status or already taking this role, those studying primary mathematics as a specialism and at Masters level, and for all primary mathematics co-ordinators.

Gina Donaldson is Senior Lecturer, Department of Postgraduate Initial Teacher Education, Canterbury Christ Church University, UK.

Jenny Field is Senior Lecturer and Coordinator of Primary Maths, University of Greenwich, UK.

Dave Harries is Teacher of Mathematics, The Wye Valley School, Buckinghamshire, UK.

Clare Tope is Mathematics Coordinator, Faculty of Education, University of Winchester, UK.

Helen Taylor is Senior Lecturer, Department of Postgraduate Initial Teacher Education, Canterbury Christ Church University, UK.

BECOMING A PRIMARY MATHEMATICS SPECIALIST TEACHER

Gina Donaldson,
Jenny Field,
Dave Harries,
Clare Tope and
Helen Taylor

Routledge
Taylor & Francis Group

LONDON AND NEW YORK

First published 2012
by Routledge
2 Park Square, Milton Park, Abingdon, Oxon OX14 4RN

Simultaneously published in the USA and Canada
by Routledge
711 Third Avenue, New York, NY 10017

Routledge is an imprint of the Taylor & Francis Group, an informa business

© 2012 Gina Donaldson, Jenny Field, Dave Harries, Clare Tope and Helen Taylor

The right of Gina Donaldson, Jenny Field, Dave Harries, Clare Tope and
Helen Taylor to be identified as authors of this work has been asserted by
them in accordance with sections 77 and 78 of the Copyright, Designs
and Patents Act 1988.

British Library Cataloguing in Publication Data
A catalogue record for this book is available from the British Library

Library of Congress Cataloging in Publication Data
Becoming a primary mathematics specialist teacher / Gina Donaldson ... [et al.].
    p. cm.
1. Mathematics—Study and teaching (Primary) 2. Teacher effectiveness.
I. Donaldson, Gina.
QA135.6.B435 2012
372.7023—dc23   2011044429

ISBN: 978-0-415-60433-8 (hbk)
ISBN: 978-0-415-60434-5 (pbk)
ISBN: 978-0-203-12059-0 (ebk)

Typeset in Times New Roman and Helvetica Neue
by Cenveo Publisher Services

MIX
Paper from
responsible sources
FSC® C004839   Printed and bound by CPI Group (UK) Ltd, Croydon, CR0 4YY

CONTENTS

LIST OF FIGURES AND TABLES

FIGURES

TABLES

INTRODUCTION

This book is written to help you to explore the role of mathematics specialist teacher in a primary school. It is written for teachers, with some experience in the classroom, who enjoy engaging children in mathematics and are excited by the prospect of learning it themselves. It will support you if you wish to develop your understanding further by exploring research and undertaking mathematical and pedagogical tasks.

Williams (2008) proposed that all schools should have access to a mathematics specialist teacher, and recommended that these teachers should develop deep mathematical knowledge, pedagogical knowledge of how mathematics is taught and learned, and the skills needed to support their colleagues. These three themes are central to this book and provide a framework for you to consider how you can change the way that mathematics is taught, and the way children enjoy and learn it.

A mathematics specialist teacher champions the teaching and learning of mathematics across the school. This may be from the early years to Year 6. You may have considerable experience of being a class teacher in some of these year groups, but most probably not in all of them. There may be areas of the primary phase where you feel less experienced and confident. We hope to offer you key ideas which will apply to your own classroom, and to other year groups across the primary phase. We intend to support you in gaining insight into the knowledge and understanding needed to develop high-quality teaching in any of these year groups, for example by helping you to identify key ideas and unpick principles of progression.

The first five chapters set the scene through a theoretical exploration of these three themes. Chapter 1 considers the nature of the role of the specialist, and Chapter 2 looks specifically at how, as the specialist, you can challenge attitudes to mathematics in your school. Chapter 3 explores the features of deep subject knowledge of primary mathematics. Chapter 4 considers the pedagogy of primary mathematics. Chapter 5 prepares you to develop the skills of coaching and mentoring to enable you to support teachers and teaching assistants in your school.

Chapters 6, 7 and 8 apply the key features of deep subject knowledge and pedagogy in three areas of the curriculum: multiplication, time and data handling. These features are therefore set in the context of specific mathematical topics, and in some cases the order of the features of deep subject knowledge and pedagogy are changed to suit the mathematical topic discussed. We have chosen these particular areas of mathematics as they represent examples of each of three key aspects of the curriculum: calculation, measures and data handling. Each area has the potential for rich mathematical discussion with both children and staff. By covering a small number of mathematical ideas in depth, we hope to enable you to apply your thinking to all areas of the mathematics curriculum. Each of these chapters asks you to consider scenarios of working with colleagues to develop their teaching of mathematics and to explore skills of mentoring and coaching.

This book is written to challenge and make explicit your beliefs and understanding of mathematics and its teaching and learning. It requires you to look deeply at practices which you might ordinarily take for granted. We refer to literature to help you to analyse the teaching and learning of mathematics in the light of new ideas. This is typical of working at Masters level, and the book is written to support you in this. Each chapter also offers you reflection activities. These may be specific mathematical tasks, designed to underpin high-quality classroom practice. Others ask you to reflect on your classroom and school, developing insights into pedagogy and leading change. You may want to discuss your learning with your colleagues, as this can deepen your reflection. The chapters also suggest further reading for you to consider particular ideas in more depth.

The National Centre for Excellence in the Teaching of Mathematics (NCETM) is a government-funded body which aims to provide a national infrastructure specifically for mathematics continuing professional development (CPD). Its online resources will support teachers in both subject knowledge and pedagogy, and we would highly recommend that you register with them to access this knowledge base.

As the mathematics specialist teacher you can make a difference by supporting colleagues, introducing new ideas, challenging or reaffirming current practices and taking a critical look at mathematics in your school. We hope you enjoy this exciting role and that the children in your school enjoy learning mathematics.

THE ROLE OF THE PRIMARY MATHEMATICS SPECIALIST TEACHER

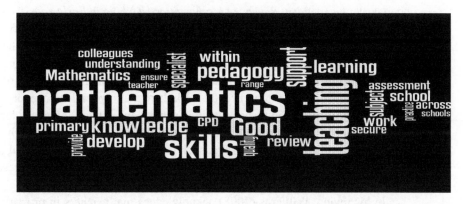

■ **Figure 1.1** A 'wordle' constructed using relevant elements of the Williams Review (2008)

INTRODUCTION

So what is the role of a mathematics specialist teacher? Perhaps you are considering yourself for this role, or have already embarked on a programme to gain this status. If you have a passion for teaching mathematics, if you want to make a difference and impact upon the continuing professional development of others, then read on … this might be the very role for you!

In this chapter we will clarify the role of the mathematics specialist teacher (MaST), for both prospective and training MaSTs, providing support and guidance as you prepare for this crucial and multifaceted status.

This chapter aims to explore the nature of the role of the subject specialist by:

1   considering how the need for mathematics specialist teachers emerged;
2   identifying the importance of subject specialists;
3   exploring the key elements of the MaST programme;

4   evaluating your future potential as a mathematics specialist teacher;
5   considering the importance of your school in providing necessary support;
6   identifying your key responsibilities in this role;
7   exploring the benefits for both the school and the mathematics specialist teacher.

HOW THE NEED FOR MATHEMATICS SPECIALIST TEACHERS EMERGED

The recent government White Paper *The Importance of Teaching* (DfE 2010: 45) clearly states a need for this role in our schools: 'We need more specialist mathematics teachers in primary schools and will encourage and support schools in developing this specialism.' It reiterates this by stating that it will focus central government support on strategic curriculum subjects, particularly mathematics and science. This provides welcome affirmation of the conclusions of the Williams Review (2008) which preceded it.

Sir Peter Williams (ibid.) was commissioned by the government at that time to undertake an *Independent Review of Mathematics Teaching in Early Years Settings and Primary Schools*. Its rationale was to review mathematics provision, to identify strengths and to focus on areas for development, making clear recommendations for the future.

Williams (2008: 1) identifies ten key recommendations which he argues will support the development of high-quality provision in mathematics. One of the key recommendations is 'the presence of a Mathematics Specialist in every primary school, who will champion this challenging subject and act as the nucleus for achieving best pedagogical practice'. Donaldson (2002) supports the need for such effective leadership in mathematics, stating that such teachers would be creative and inspiring in their teaching ... lessons would be exciting, motivating and intriguing, resulting in increased enthusiasm and raising the profile of mathematics.

In his review Williams (2008) acknowledges that teachers in primary schools are not normally 'Mathematics Specialists' and he argues that this needs to change. This idea was previously raised almost 30 years ago by Cockroft (1982: 199), reporting to the government of that time. He also highlighted this issue, focusing on 'mathematical expertise which is so badly needed in primary schools' and a real necessity to ensure that primary teachers with mathematical expertise are appointed.

The process of moving forward with this finally began in September 2009, as a direct result of Williams' 'Recommendation 3': that 'There should be at least one Mathematics Specialist in each primary school ... with deep mathematical subject and pedagogical knowledge' (2008: 25). As a consequence of this key recommendation, the government invited higher education institutions to offer a national Masters-level training programme, and thus emerged the Mathematics Specialist Teacher Status, commonly known as MaST.

THE IMPORTANCE OF SUBJECT SPECIALISTS

The Royal Society's report (2010: 2) summarising the key issues in primary mathematics states that teaching specialisms are not generally recorded across the UK, but that 'it is society's view that this situation needs to change if children are going to be given the best possible start'. It reiterates this by clearly identifying an 'urgent need' to find ways of providing post-qualification routes to acquiring specialisms 'such as the Mathematics Specialist Teacher primary programme' (p. 3), seeing this as a clear way to improve quality. In its evidence-based approach to supporting responsible policy-making within education it states that the 'Masters-level qualifications that have been established in England to develop mathematics "specialists" in primary schools need to be sustained' (p. 4) and goes on to list this as an 'Action' for on-going commitment.

Ofsted had supported this view two years earlier. In its report into mathematics, *Understanding the Score* (2008: 7), it recommends that the government should 'explore strategies through which the subject expertise ... can be developed and lead to recognition and reward ... enhancing the role of subject leader for mathematics so that teachers aspire to it'. It also placed responsibility on schools, stating that they should improve their own subject leader's expertise, placing an important emphasis on a 'home grown' attitude to CPD.

Even before this Askew *et al.* (1997: 94), researching into effective teachers of numeracy, produced evidence that extended CPD programmes (which would describe the MaST programme) 'were perceived by teachers as highly influential in developing their beliefs and practice' and gave rise to real improvements in the classroom. This led to the question 'should extended programmes of CPD in mathematics education have priority and if so who should provide them and what components should they contain?' We are very glad to say that the MaST programme has now been seen as a key priority, and we will now discuss the components of this programme.

THE KEY ELEMENTS OF THE MaST PROGRAMME

One of the major factors, paramount in improving the teaching of mathematics, is tackling the issue of attitudes. This will be comprehensively dealt with in Chapter 2; however it is crucial to state here that positive attitudes towards mathematics will be central to becoming a successful MaST, and essential in maximising success in each of the three key elements of this training programme.

Fraser and Honeyford (2000: 1) state that 'one of the issues facing many primary teachers charged with teaching mathematics is that they do not like mathematics ... and do not feel confident teaching it'. Haylock (2010: 10) adds to this, stating that 'amongst many primary school teachers in general, there is this background of anxiety and confusion', and promoting positive attitudes is a 'major task'. Therefore, to have any real impact, developing positive attitudes in all your colleagues would need to be central to your philosophy. Little real progress could be made in the three key elements discussed below without this first being in place.

As a mathematics specialist teacher you must 'champion' your subject. You must be prepared to tackle and change negative attitudes. To a large extent this will be driven by your own enthusiasm for the subject; passion breeds passion, excitement breeds excitement – without doubt attitudes are contagious!

Now with this positivity firmly in place we can explore the *three key elements* that inform the programme:

1   The development of deep mathematical *subject knowledge* from EYFS to KS3, with a clear understanding of progression in key areas.
2   The development of a wide repertoire of *subject-specific pedagogy* with a clear understanding of how these teaching approaches enable children to learn.
3   A developing ability to *mentor and coach others*, sharing your expertise and providing whole-school impact through classroom-based collaborative professional development.

Deep mathematical subject knowledge

This will be investigated in much more detail in Chapter 3; however, an outline is provided here to establish a context. As a MaST you will be confident and happy to both review your own emerging subject knowledge needs and those of others, promoting the attitude of 'always learning' within your school. The knowledge you have gained through this programme will enable you to provide support to your colleagues in improving their own subject knowledge needs once identified.

At the end of your training you will be expected to have developed a clear understanding of progression in key mathematical concepts from EYFS to KS3 and to be confident to teach across age phases. It is therefore hoped that you will feel able to offer advice to all staff accordingly, with both their planning and teaching. In fact we have not been surprised to find that many teachers on the programme feel confident within their own year group: 'I have been teaching in Year 6 for many years now'; however they lack confidence when considering what goes on in other places in the school: 'I'm scared of going into the nursery. Staff there don't think I know anything about it! They smile and say "get back to Year 6" … they're right, I don't.' It therefore delights us when, some months on, they confidently and enthusiastically lead meetings on the principles of counting – especially when their early years staff are so impressed and go on to change their approaches as a result!

Of course, centrally important *is* the ability to demonstrate a clear conceptual understanding of key mathematical principles and, crucially, the connections between them. Haylock (2010: 9) suggests that this 'involves knowing how fractions relate to whole numbers, where they belong on a number line, how they link to … ratio and proportion, the connections between fractions and the division operations'. A MaST will develop a strong conceptual understanding, which will bring to fruition a rich tapestry of connections, exposing true understanding for the learner.

In addition to understanding how concepts inter-relate within mathematics is the importance of cross-curricular and real-life application. You will increase your understanding of the importance of using and applying mathematics, and making it more relevant to staff and children alike. This will include becoming more familiar with key aspects of learning, which include problem solving, reasoning and enquiry, and promoting this across your school.

Although subject knowledge per se is vital, a report by Ofsted (2008) talks about effective teaching relying on essential ingredients which include both subject knowledge and understanding the ways in which pupils learn mathematics – drawn together to form 'subject expertise'. This leads neatly into the next key element.

Subject-specific pedagogy

A specific focus on pedagogy forms the content of Chapter 4, but an outline is provided here. The crucial issue here may well be an understanding that subject knowledge alone is not enough. A wide and appropriate range of subject-specific pedagogy for the teaching and learning of mathematics is vital. You will need a critical awareness of experiential learning, alongside a developing range of models and images that will support and promote children's conceptual understanding, in addition to a clear understanding of when to withdraw practical resources and encourage abstract reasoning.

Identification and analysis of misconceptions will also form part of your developing entourage of pedagogy; of course it is one thing to recognise a misconception, but a more skilled approach will allow you to establish why it has arisen and how best it can be exposed and addressed. In many cases teachers who wish to be specialists could indeed be re-learning certain areas of the mathematics curriculum. They may well become aware that their own teaching has unwittingly encouraged the development of such misconceptions.

Developing a more secure knowledge of subject-specific pedagogy will also enable you to set up rich opportunities to assess children's knowledge and learning. Through 'transformative listening' (Williams 2008) you will change direction and adapt your teaching to suit the individual needs of your class – and of course you will support colleagues to do the same.

The Cambridge Review (Alexander 2009) talks about a pedagogy of repertoire, rather than a pedagogy of recipe, and of principle instead of prescription. Haylock (2010: 10) supports this view, stating that we need to move 'away from the notion of teaching a recipe and more towards developing understanding'. These are timely statements to reflect upon, as we move away from the strategies, which having set us on our way and supported many, can now make room for a more creative curriculum. As a MaST you will support and develop this 'repertoire' of pedagogy, encouraging risk taking, decision making, exploration and justification of choices made, breathing life back into the curriculum and with it an enthusiasm which many sorely lack.

Mentoring and coaching

Chapter 5 will provide you with more detailed information on aspects of mentoring and coaching. We understand that this is an area which may be less familiar to many of you at the start of the course. You may feel less sure and ask yourself: how will I make an impact? How will I find the time? How will I deal with that challenging member of staff who does not like to listen? An important part of the training programme considers the answers to these, and other similar questions.

Mentoring and coaching is indeed crucial if the notion of 'specialist teacher' is to succeed. As a MaST, everything you have learned in terms of subject knowledge and pedagogy is of limited use unless you are able to share it with others. Being a MaST is not mainly about your own classroom practice, but your ability to share it with others and make a difference within your school to the mathematics provision for all children. Therefore the third crucial element is one of mentoring and coaching, enabling you to share good practice and promote whole-school impact.

Any coaching or mentoring support needs to be informed by a real understanding of the best approaches to school-based professional development. Relevant research into key approaches to mentoring and coaching will need to form an integral part of training, as well as barriers to making progress.

As a MaST you will be able to support your colleagues in a number of ways, both during your training programme and once qualified. Primarily and crucially your role will be to create enthusiasm for the subject where it is lacking, to 'champion' mathematics and have a determination to change attitudes, where necessary, among staff, children and parents.

This positivity will create an environment which facilitates learning. This will enable you to help colleagues to audit their subject knowledge and their understanding of progression, and provide the relevant support where areas of need are identified. In addition, you will be able to strengthen pedagogical practice within your school – leading by example and sharing good practice through targeted practical professional development.

Staff will be supported in the identification of misconceptions and misunderstandings in mathematics, and the best ways to address them to enhance the learning process. This will lead to a more inclusive policy – where teachers are able to plan for the needs of all children.

As part of your Masters-level study, you will actively 'engage with research' (Williams 2008: 24). The combination of engaging with relevant research, alongside your own classroom practice and the time to reflect, will enable you to promote thoughtful, high-quality mathematics teaching throughout your school. This will be strengthened by the fact that it is evidence-based and firmly rooted in academic research; such an approach will establish a fruitful learning environment.

The Advisory Committee for Mathematics Education (ACME) (2005) said that CPD was most effective when it involved those who encouraged and influenced others; people who could increase levels of confidence and self esteem in others and help them to tackle new challenges. What is also most crucial here is the importance of learning together. It certainly won't always go right. You might decide to hold a 'things that went wrong' meeting, and be prepared to lead with one of your own examples! Or you might take a topic within mathematics and consider how each member of staff would approach it, what progression would look like and what misconceptions might occur. Most importantly remember that this is a shared learning journey and a joint venture for the MaST, leadership team, all staff, children and parents.

With that in mind it is also important to say that all this will only prove really successful where you have the support of the leadership team. For a school to get the best out of a specialist teacher both school and teacher must be committed to it. The leadership team must see both its relevance and importance in taking your school forward. This will enable you to both shape future mathematics staff provision and monitor whole-school impact.

Reflective task

You are now aware of the three key features of MaST.

Where do you believe your strengths lie within these three key elements?

Can you already identify areas for your own professional development?

Are you interested to learn more?

WOULD YOU MAKE A GOOD MATHEMATICS SPECIALIST TEACHER?

Askew *et al.* (1997), researching into effective teachers of numeracy, ask how effective teachers of numeracy already in schools can be better identified. This section aims to enable you to identify if this *is* indeed the role for you, and whether at some future point you will be able to spread your expertise among others.

At the start of the programme

As a prospective mathematics specialist teacher you will be highly motivated and committed to making a change. At the start of the programme you will be a good classroom practitioner with a keen interest in primary maths and a thirst to make a change. You will see a clear need to engage children in their own learning. DCSF (2009: 166) emphasise this with great clarity: 'don't expect children to be interested in mathematics if you don't share an interest and all their mathematics is dull'. As a prospective specialist teacher you will also be acutely aware of this.

It is also essential that you have good inter-personal skills which will allow you to support colleagues in a friendly and enthusiastic manner. Donaldson (2002) describes successful mathematics leadership as creating a climate which enables other staff to develop the confidence to teach it. You will be someone who promotes certain beliefs and demonstrates positive practices, and in doing so will be able to create a climate where teachers feel able to learn and reflect without feeling vulnerable. Of course your own ability to reflect will also be vital. This will enable you to analyse at a deeper level both your own practice and that of others.

In addition, at the start of the programme good subject knowledge and effective pedagogy will be important, but equally important is a willingness to improve further

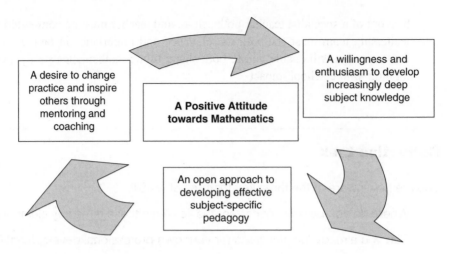

■ **Figure 1.2** Attributes as you begin your journey towards MaST status

and recognise any gaps. Donaldson (2002) argues that effective training courses can convince teachers to change their practice. As an integral part of the programme, undertaking your training with so many other talented teachers, you will find that learning will be reciprocal and support groups can be established.

A mathematics specialist would not necessarily be the mathematics co-ordinator in the school, therefore opening up opportunities for those interested in developing mathematics but not holding a co-ordinator's post. However, they would need to have a good working relationship with the school leadership team, as previously stated.

If you are considering the role of mathematics specialist teacher within your school, you are already likely to be committed to your own continuing professional development, and you will enjoy undertaking the work involved in the programme. Figure 1.2 summarises the attributes of a potential mathematics specialist.

At the end of the programme

Once you have gained mathematics specialist status your personal and professional characteristics are likely to include:

■ a secure and deeper understanding of subject knowledge and subject-specific pedagogy;
■ a much more detailed understanding and knowledge of progression across all age phases;
■ a clear and defined role as coach and mentor within your school – leading collaborative professional development and aiming to improve provision;
■ an ability to encourage and promote high-quality, lively mathematic provision throughout your school – leading by example and demonstrating positive attitudes and enthusiasm;

■   an ability to support your colleagues and help them to develop and improve their practice and their understanding of the ways in which children best learn mathematics;

■   an understanding of the importance of drawing upon research to support class-based professional development;

■   an ability to help colleagues identify misconceptions and diagnose mis-understandings, and through this assessment improve future planning for all children;

■   a clear direction, working with your leadership team to evaluate the impact of your role within the school and design future provision.

At this point we would like to challenge you to think very personally about the MaST role, and the possible impact you could have as a 'mathematics champion' within your school. We are sure you will have concluded that the role of the maths specialist teacher is multifaceted, so perhaps now would be a good time to reflect on Figure 1.3 to ascertain whether you feel this really could be the role for you.

It is important to clarify that each of the three inner attributes in Figure 1.3 should continue to develop throughout our teaching careers. Maths specialist teachers may well have developed high skills in each of these areas, but their journey for the acquisition of knowledge is never complete! After many years of teaching, many of which have been dedicated solely to primary mathematics, as authors we can happily say that we still find ourselves questioning our own subject knowledge at times, and eagerly receive new ideas which we all feel will bring engagement and motivation to the lives of others. Indeed, our best teachers are those who freely admit there is always room for improvement.

A sobering thought then could be that of Lewis (1996: 176), who says 'There is no point at which teachers become perfect', in fact having the self confidence to enjoy *not* always knowing, being willing to learn, trying things out, using your imagination ... that's what really matters.

As we have previously expressed, a positive attitude to mathematics is the starting point which encompasses all the other attributes. If you can confidently put yourself within this outer circle, with a willingness to inspire others and a keenness to learn more – you have the essential characteristics which are crucial for those first steps towards MaST status. This positive attitude will provide support as you further develop your knowledge in each of the three other areas.

Reflective task

Do you feel this is a journey you would like to take?

Can you already identify staff that you know would want to come along with you?

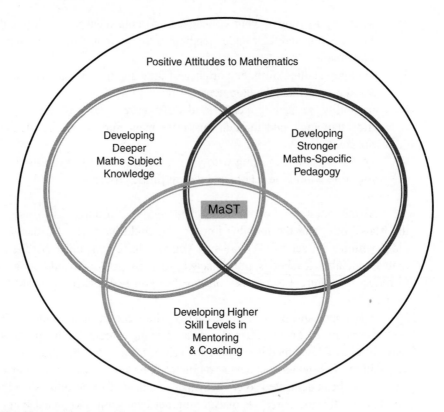

■ **Figure 1.3** Attributes of a mathematics specialist teacher

HOW COULD YOUR SCHOOL SUPPORT YOU?

For your school to reap the maximum benefit from selecting and training a mathematics specialist teacher, the role should form an integral part of the whole school's development plan, setting out to improve teaching and raise attainment in mathematics. Williams (2008: 4) endorses this, saying 'of paramount importance to this strategy are the Head teacher, senior management team and the school governors' and 'successful delivery of CPD is dependent on strong leadership in the school' (p. 6). Further evidence is provided by 'The Pathfinder Project' which preceded MaST. It found that the best outcomes for both school and specialist teacher occurred when the head teacher was part of the process and fully endorsed it.

To be truly successful you *will* need support from your school's senior leadership team. They will need to demonstrate a strong, clear commitment to on-going long-term school improvements in maths. This leadership team should recognise the value of collaborative classroom-based professional development. The National Centre for Excellence in the Teaching of Mathematics (NCETM: see https://www.ncetm.org.uk) acknowledges this, setting out the essential role of senior management in enabling the learning of the MaST to 'extend beyond their own practice' and impact upon colleagues throughout the school.

The leadership team needs to make provision for the release of the MaST to work alongside other teachers if real benefit is to be gained from this resource. Askew *et al.* (1997: 4) argue that even highly effective mathematics co-ordinators will not significantly influence other teachers without sufficient time to do so. In their research they found that in schools where staffing allowed for this, there was evidence of 'significantly higher numeracy standards than in comparable schools'. Without doubt this is of paramount importance if this process is to succeed.

THE RESPONSIBILITIES OF A MATHEMATICS SPECIALIST

Reflective task

Do you believe your leadership team would relish this challenge?

Do you feel that you could get support to develop your role?

TEACHER

We expect that at this point you would like some specific details of what such a role might include. With this in mind we have set out to list some of the activities that might well form part of your role in schools.

An overview of the larger picture here would include:

■ working with the staff in your school to identify their needs in terms of both subject knowledge and pedagogy;
■ working alongside the leadership team to provide high-quality CPD for staff which supports staff and improves standards within your school;
■ creating positive attitudes to mathematics, generating enthusiasm in staff, children and parents and raising the profile of mathematics;
■ where appropriate providing support for NQTs, ITE students and teaching assistants within your school.

More specific ideas to promote collaborative professional development would include:

■ team-teaching an area of mathematics;
■ undertaking a subject knowledge audit, such as those on the NCETM website, with a colleague and using this to identify and work on subject knowledge needs;

- discussing ideas such as visual models, images and resources or an approach to teaching mathematics which has been covered in the course, with a colleague. Agreeing with the colleague to try out this approach and meeting later to discuss its impact;
- observing a teacher's lesson (at their request) to improve practice in specific areas you have both identified;
- providing a lesson for another teacher to observe, perhaps providing a specific focus such as mathematics dialogue, analysing children's errors or promoting problem-solving approaches;
- joint planning of an area of mathematics and reviewing progress together afterwards;
- analysing a selection of children's work across the school in an area of mathematics to highlight issues of progression and continuity of, for example, the use of vocabulary and visual images;
- providing staff meetings and 'mini' meetings based on specific needs identified by the school and the MaST;
- providing professional development to teaching assistants;
- joint planning and leading a lesson study, focusing on an area of mathematics or mathematics teaching and learning identified as a priority for the school.

(Adapted from an unpublished DfE Mathematics
Specialist Programme Discussion Paper)

Reflective task

Maybe you will feel that you already have responsibility for some of these aspects within your school?

Perhaps you will be able to identify others you would like to develop further?

Or you may have done very little, but be keen to 'get stuck in'!

WHAT ARE THE BENEFITS FOR BOTH THE SCHOOL AND THE MATHEMATICS SPECIALIST TEACHER?

A most encouraging thing about training to be a specialist teacher is that you will find that you have both something to offer and equally something to gain. You can therefore make a difference for both yourself and others – a 'win-win' situation!

Williams (2008) sets out these benefits for both the mathematics specialist and the school as a whole (see Tables 1.1 and 1.2).

■ Table 1.1 Identifying the benefits of becoming a mathematics specialist teacher

Benefits for the mathematics specialist	Benefits for the school/head teacher
More confident and able to develop enthusiasm across the school for learning mathematics	Access to recent research into effective teaching and learning practices, which can be disseminated through your school
Improved mathematical subject knowledge and subject-specific pedagogical skills with increased effectiveness	Opportunity to develop a key member of staff who can lead professional development and in-school mathematics CPD that is accessible to all the teaching and support staff
Improved understanding of progression from EYFS to end of KS2, increasing your confidence in addressing and supporting all staff	Mathematics professional support available through mentoring to trainees or newly qualified staff, or coaching to teachers or teaching assistants
Enhanced use of assessment-for-learning strategies and the planning of targeted intervention	Mathematics champion in the school who can generate enthusiasm for learning the subject among children, parents and staff
Good understanding of the importance of research-based enquiry and using it as part of the teaching and learning process	More opportunities to explore and take forward informed in-school collaborative research in mathematics
Access to and knowledge of CPD opportunities in mathematics that could support colleagues in your school	Informed advice about the mathematical professional needs of the staff in your school and the range of CPD opportunities available that can inform school planning and self-evaluation processes
Opportunities to develop professionally and gain formal status and Masters-level qualification	
Opportunities to be part of a local authority network and access to support structures	
Opportunities to join a national network of other mathematics specialist teachers to discuss your practice and share ideas	

Adapted from Williams (2008: 26)

■ Table 1.2 Specific benefits identified by our current trainees

Benefits to my teaching	Benefits to staff	Benefits to the whole school
I consider how I can make tasks richer and more engaging	Staff have come up to me and said 'wow that really works and the children are starting to get it'	The school has been monitoring the impact of my work relating to children's attainment – positive results so far!
I have moved well away from schemes and spend more time discussing and talking with children rather than *at* them	Going into a year 1 class and looking at questioning – I was able to model for another teacher	Improved subject knowledge has helped me to develop a school vision for mathematics and develop staff training sessions effectively for colleagues

(continued)

Benefits to my teaching	Benefits to staff	Benefits to the whole school
Haven't stopped talking about Saturday since the time I left. You inspire such confidence just wanted to say thank you I thought yesterday's session on Algebra was great Real academic discussion based on reading has developed my pedagogy I have introduced new resources to make my maths lessons more interactive Use of errors and misconceptions as a focus for teaching. I now openly expose and explore misconceptions with the children I have a much greater understanding of how to make connections between areas of mathematics and how to address misconceptions I have a greater bank of rich activities that I have tried to use to develop children's learning I have changed my practice to give children more choices in their learning Have become more confident in my delivery and am taking more risks to challenge pupils My questioning has developed so that I ask questions which develop reasoning	The main positive has been informal working with all colleagues. Teachers consult with me on a regular basis about issues in their class I have worked with a colleague in my year group planning and implementing intervention strategies to support particular groups of children I have worked with staff I haven't previously – building more of a relationship and open dialogue Teachers talk to me about interesting things that have happened in their class A colleague who had previously been very unsure about maths is now leading the way in using rich mathematical tasks Empowering – have focused discussions with staff Feedback to colleagues improves practice of others	MaST has given me an increased profile and as a result colleagues discuss mathematical issues with me and contribute and believe in the school vision As a result of my own increased interest I have generally been more proactive in raising the profile of issues in mathematics I have monitored maths teaching across the school and put together an action plan to address key areas I have worked with the leadership team to develop areas that we need to improve. I am beginning to see a raised profile of mathematics in school My confidence and passion for the subject has grown, this will impact positively on the whole school

Adapted from South East Consortium Teacher Evaluations and Reflections

Reflective task

Do these benefits interest you?

Which ones interest you the most and why?

CONCLUSIONS

Government minister Ed Balls was clearly very positive about this role in 2008 when he stated that every school will have a 'maths champion' acting as a mentor and coach: as well as being an outstanding classroom practitioner, 'they will have a dramatic impact, bring excitement to maths for every teacher and child in their school' (*Guardian* 2008).

You may be forgiven for perhaps considering that this is rather a 'big ask'; however, taking small steps will get you there, and you may well enjoy the journey! Imagine throwing a pebble into the water; where the pebble enters the water produces the strongest waves, but much further away there will still be some impact as the ripples disperse. This may well symbolise your effectiveness – with some staff happy to get closest to the pebble and gain the strongest impact, while others stand back a little at first, watching and waiting to catch a wave!

Encouragingly, the NCETM describes the MaST programme as very successful, stating that primary teachers say it is 'the best CPD I have ever had'. This government-funded body actively supports MaST, providing specific areas and communities for sharing and learning within its website. This evaluation of the programme's impact is supported by those providing the programme across the country, where areas for celebration include improved teacher confidence, understanding of progression and clear whole-school impact (ITT Maths Network Meeting July 2011), and further substantiated by the DfE (2010) in a communication from the Deputy Director from the 'Improving Pupil Performance Unit': 'Ministers recognise the role that Mathematics Specialist Teachers play in improving the teaching and learning of mathematics.'

Hopefully you may now agree that in many ways this role cannot be commended enough. Reassuringly, the recent government White Paper *The Importance of Teaching* (2010: 45) reveals that the government plans to support an increase in the numbers of specialist teachers and to up-skill existing teachers: 'We need more specialist mathematics teachers in primary schools and will encourage and support schools in developing this specialism.' It is our hope that your school will soon benefit from having a mathematics specialist teacher of its own … you!

So let us now continue our journey by expanding on that very key issue which must be addressed before all others can develop … attitudes towards mathematics. How do attitudes form and why are they so important? As a MaST you will have the crucial role of inspiring others and developing positive attitudes within your whole school; we therefore dedicate the next chapter to 'attitudes to mathematics'.

Reflective task

Do you believe you could make a difference?

Having read this chapter do you feel you could have something to offer your staff, children and parents?

Then read on.

FURTHER READING

OFSTED (2010a) *Finnish Pupils' Success in Mathematics.* Manchester: Ofsted. This report provides valuable insight into why Finland has successful outcomes in mathematics.

CHAPTER 2

ATTITUDES TO MATHEMATICS

INTRODUCTION

This chapter aims to explore why attitudes towards mathematics are generally so poor in Britain. It will encourage you to reflect on the immense effect this can have on the teaching and learning of mathematics, and to consider both the consequences of this and its possible solutions by:

1   exploring our society's general attitudes towards mathematics
2   examining why it is so important that these general attitudes change
3   considering how such attitudes may have evolved:
    a   the contribution of popular culture and the British media
    b   adults' reflections on their childhood experiences
    c   parental influence over developing attitudes
4   exploring the difficulties experienced by some of our primary school teachers
5   reflecting on the way forward and how you can play a part in affecting change.

Reflective task

During a casual staff room conversation a member of staff declares 'I really don't like maths ... I have always hated teaching it.'

How would you respond?

We will ask you to revisit this at the end of the chapter.

WHAT ARE SOCIETY'S GENERAL ATTITUDES TOWARDS MATHEMATICS?

Britain doesn't like maths! Okay, so this *is* rather a strong statement, and of course there are clearly those with alternative views, but there is much evidence to support the fact that many people in our society really *do* feel this way. Almost 30 years ago a survey cited in Cockroft (1982) concluded that British adults had widespread anxiety about mathematics and felt inadequate. In fact half of those approached simply refused to participate once they were aware that the subject was mathematics. Eighteen years on, research by Lim and Ernest (2000) exploring images, beliefs and attitudes found that very little had changed, with reactions including 'No! I am not good at maths, please don't ask me anything' and the majority of those surveyed perceiving mathematics to be difficult or boring.

Sadly we have no reason to believe that current views have changed. Williams (2008: 3), in his candid report to the government, went further, saying 'The United Kingdom is still one of the few advanced nations where it is socially acceptable – fashionable even – to profess an inability to cope with the subject.' In his report to government he calls for an urgent shift to reverse the 'can't do' attitude towards mathematics, saying that every child should leave school without a fear of maths.

Negative attitudes pervade society. Fraser and Honeyford (2000: v) suggest that it appears quite respectable to say 'I cannot do mathematics' concluding that 'not being able to do mathematics is almost seen as a sign of the civilised person'. The Royal Society (2010: 5) discuss the 'need to chip away at the ingrained negative attitudes', suggesting that the 'prevailing view that it is somehow "cool" to be bad at mathematics is systematic of a cultural deficit that needs to be overturned'.

Headington (2001: 2) corroborates that failure in maths is accepted as normal, and those who succeed are somehow seen as 'different'. Although it is socially acceptable to say 'I'm hopeless at adding' we are less likely to hear someone admit 'I'm hopeless at reading.' Some years ago this was affirmed by a local authority mathematics advisor who said 'people always come up to me at courses and say with ease "I can't do maths" yet it does not happen to my colleagues on the literacy team ... no one smiles and says "I don't read well"'. So we must ask ourselves is this really down to ability, or the result of popular culture? Ofsted (1997) describes with concern our culture's readier acceptance of innumeracy than illiteracy. Many British people, even the well educated, often openly de-value and underestimate their mathematical ability.

As an example of the differences in how people perceive mathematics compared with subjects like English, let's consider the challenge of reading Chaucer. Geoffrey Chaucer was a fourteenth-century English poet who wrote in Middle English, so reading his work is certainly difficult for many, yet most do not relate this to their own lack of intelligence or to illiteracy, but rather that it *is* indeed a challenging task. Given a similar situation in mathematics, perhaps presented with a quadratic equation, reactions are likely to be much more personal and relate to ability rather than the level of the challenge: 'Oh I can't understand this, I'm hopeless at maths.' Ed Balls, in an article in the *Guardian* (17 July 2008), spoke of government determination to address this stark observation that it is acceptable to admit to being poor at maths.

The National Centre for Excellence in the Teaching of Mathematics (NCETM), a government-funded CPD provider, strongly suggests that these attitudes are specific to our English culture and are not universal. It describes a situation where a group of academics from England and Poland met at a conference. Discussion turned to mathematics, and an English academic said 'Oh, I can't do maths to save my life!' which was followed by sympathetic laughter from others in the English party, but the Poles sat 'stony faced and visibly shocked', then expressed surprise at such a public admission: 'I have to say it is very embarrassing.' It was then pointed out to them that in English society it is very acceptable and in fact meant you were a 'good egg'. Research by Lim and Ernest (2000: 193) affirms this scenario: 'adults in Anglo-American countries are not embarrassed to proclaim their ignorance'.

There are other examples which point to differing world-wide attitudes. Carol Vorderman, a television personality renowned by the general public for her mathematical ability, said 'there is no question that those from an Indian or Asian background and many from Eastern Europe, respect and revel in the subject' (*Guardian* 2008), and research by Drew and Hansen (2007) into the Western Australian Curriculum finds a whole area devoted to 'Appreciating Mathematics'. It would be challenging to find a corresponding element in our own National Curriculum. This makes worrying reading when we are living and competing in an ever-growing global market.

But is anything likely to change when these views 'are regularly rehearsed by the media, in pubs and in the school playground'? (NCETM), and why is change so important?

Reflective task

What can we learn from the approaches of other cultures?

Do you consider that our general attitudes could be putting us behind the rest of the civilised world?

WHY IT IS *SO* IMPORTANT THAT THESE GENERAL ATTITUDES CHANGE?

To answer this question it is crucial to understand that attitudes do affect learning. Katz (1995) argues that 'disposition' influences learning, and this is often reflected through perseverance and the speed at which children give up. Skemp (1989) also believes that negative emotions greatly influence learning, and a recent study by Ashcroft and Moore (2009) points to findings that anxiety takes up working memory space, leading to a drop in performance. This all leads to the worrying conclusion that negativity affects numeracy; and too many British adults are functionally innumerate.

When Cockroft (1982: 5) raised this issue in his report to government, saying that 'functional innumeracy is far more widespread than anyone has cared to believe', it did cause concern. However, almost three decades on it is difficult to identify any real progress, with recent government figures revealing that 6.8 million workers in Britain today are 'functionally innumerate' (*Daily Telegraph* 5 June 2008), *more even* than the number of those who are illiterate.

A lack of functional mathematics in society is certainly an issue. Examples of this are all around us, from staff in shops who cannot calculate 10 per cent without a calculator, to adults who are unable to perform mental maths and resort to putting one number on top of the other 'in their heads'. Interestingly, it is often the older generation who demonstrate most frustration with this. Houssart (2007: 10) records some damming opinions of the elderly: 'I am appalled at the inability of younger people to use figures' (Jack, aged 83); 'they don't use their BRAINS, what a pity' (Winnie, aged 82).

Let us stop for a moment to consider the price paid by many individuals as a direct result of their innumeracy. Haylock (2010: 5) reports that these adults 'viewed themselves as failures'. The damaging effect this has on confidence is one thing, but what about their inability to function or thrive? The NCETM (2010c) recently produced these sobering statistics: 'more than a fifth of adults in the UK do not have the basic numeracy skills needed for the complexities of modern everyday life'; these include household budgeting, understanding interest rates, interpreting statistical information and helping children with homework. This can have a 'dramatic effect' on life chances, with data illustrating that they are twice as likely to be unemployed.

In stark contrast, those with better numeracy skills are 'more likely to own their own homes, have savings and are less likely to be on benefits'. The government's statutory requirements set out in *Every Child Matters* make it clear that education should enable the adults of tomorrow to stay safe, live purposeful lives and make a positive contribution to society; so you may well agree with the NCETM (2010a) that this could be interpreted as an equal opportunities issue.

As we have seen, at an individual level this is a real cause for concern, but what about the effects on Britain as a whole? The costs to society of an innumerate population is considerable, in fact running into billions of pounds: 'With one quarter of national GDP resulting from the mathematics based financial services sector, the importance of mathematics in general hardly needs stating' (Williams 2008: 32). Carol Vorderman (*Guardian* 2008) supports this view:

> whether you like it or not, and no matter what the … fashion of the day may be, the basis of our global future is one built on science and computing and manufacturing and hard business, and the language they all use is mathematics.

The recent government White Paper *The Importance of Teaching* (2010) makes for uneasy reading, stating that employers continue to report shortages in mathematical skills and that Britain's school system is performing well below its potential and can significantly improve. In fact many countries in the world are improving faster than we are; the latest report by the World Economic Forum (2011) ranks the quality of mathematics and science education in the UK as 43rd in the world, behind countries such as Iran and Lithuania.

However, it would be unfair not to recognise success over recent years. Williams (2008) reports that since the introduction of the National Numeracy Strategies, 83,000 more 11-year-olds are reaching the required level and TIMSS (Trends in International Mathematics and Science Study) (2007) finds that England's students are among some of the best in the world. However, this must be considered alongside the fact that by Year 9 only 40 per cent enjoy mathematics, and 150,000 pupils leave primary school without being fully numerate. In addition, research by Albone and Tymms (2004) into the impact of the strategies demonstrates a year-on-year decline in children's attitudes.

So if the acquisition of negative attitudes influences learning, leading to higher levels of innumeracy, then it is important to consider the root of them. Being able to establish a cause will have significant bearing on future actions and may empower us to act as facilitators of change. Let us explore further.

HOW HAVE SUCH ATTITUDES EVOLVED?

The attitudes of a society are not formed in an instant; shared experiences over time will contribute to general opinions, and this in turn will lead to a consensus, which becomes self-perpetuating. We aim to explore what may have led to these general opinions about mathematics, and how they could be both 'learned' and 'experiential'.

Lim (2002), researching into public images of mathematics, suggests that there may well be major influencing factors, and identifies these as: parents, teachers, school experiences and, in addition, social and cultural factors. Hannula (2002) considers four aspects to be important in forming attitudes: present experiences; past experiences; pre-conceived ideas; and future life goals. Reflecting on this, we have identified three major factors which we believe to be influential.

The contribution of popular culture and the British media

In an article in the *Guardian* (17 June 2008) Carol Vorderman expressed strong views about how media influences society as a whole: 'we hear, to the point of boredom, on children's TV, on soaps, on news and daytime shows "oh I'm rubbish at maths" or "you're a nerd"'. The media plays a large part in raising 'the spectre of our negative cultural attitude'. It is certainly true to say that 'the mathematician' is often depicted as the 'geek' in popular culture, and it could be argued that this *is* a 'turn off' for many British teenagers.

It is easy to substantiate the view that the media is a contributing factor. You will find you can quickly collect examples when you home in on them; like the popular supermarket chain advertising its calculators by suggesting that they would make maths 'less scary': what about those children who had not thought that maths was scary up until that point? Or an intelligent actress on a popular chat show, happily explaining how she is unable to cope with her young child's maths homework?

Recent 'throw away' statements to audiences of millions range from a respected television presenter exclaiming 'even *I* can work out the maths' to a powerful main character in a popular film exclaiming 'I hate maths!' Even a recent 'light holiday read' concluded that the main character would kill herself if she was not able to 'out glam' the mathematicians at her brother's wedding! Through popular culture people are often categorised as either creative or mathematical, as if it is impossible to be both. Yes, it is worryingly easy to form such a collection of anecdotal evidence; begin to listen out for them yourself!

It is likely that those in the 'limelight' have not considered that they are perpetuating negative images, or that this would matter very much anyway; in fact they *themselves* are victims of society's attitudes. However, these people do affect us! We care what 'celebrities' have to say and many people adapt their views accordingly. It may well be time for those in positions of influence to act more responsibly, and for the media to be accountable for the reinforcement of these negative stereotypes.

Adults' reflections on their childhood experiences

It must be remembered that although the media reinforces and perpetuates negativity, it did not create it. Many adults cite their school days as the root of their bad relationship with mathematics, with many carrying around emotional baggage for years. This is most often associated with poor teaching and humiliating classroom experiences

Suggate *et al.* (2010: 2) confirm this, saying, 'It has often been suggested, rather uncharitably, that the subject attracts a disproportionate number of teachers lacking perception and insight' and that incompetent and insensitive teaching can lead to adults who are 'mentally scarred by past experience of failure'. Buxton (1981) also describes mathematics as having its fair share of teachers who lack patience, do not explain well and who use their own understanding to belittle others. Cockburn (1999) argues that it is also possible for a teacher to know too much maths and not be able to relate to the difficulties of others. We would like to think that all this is perhaps overly harsh on our profession; however, social history proves that it certainly does have some foundations in the truth.

Further research by Lim and Ernest (2000: 205) finds that adults have very strong opinions about learning mathematics, with some describing it as like 'having a tooth pulled out'. Analysis of data *again* suggests that a major influence in the formation of these images was memories of a particular mathematics teacher:

> I remember when I was seven I had to do a hundred long divisions. The head master came in ... He picked me up and banged me up and down on my chair saying 'Why can't you do it?' After that I wouldn't ask if I couldn't understand something.
>
> (Haylock 2010: 7)

Cockburn (1999: 12) summarises this, saying 'if a child has the potential to be a brilliant mathematician ... but is terrified of the teacher he or she may well find it hard to perform'. This is also a key finding by Williams (2008: 6): 'It is a central conclusion of this review that the teacher ... determines learning outcomes in mathematics.'

Skemp (1989) concludes that 'fear' is one of the greatest emotions. He describes the type of teacher who shouts louder and thumps on the table to emphasise points if asked to explain again; this approach is not conducive to clear thinking. Haylock (2010: 6) confirms that these expressions of 'fear' are by no means out of the ordinary: 'Maths struck terror in my heart; a real fear that has stayed with me from over 20 years ago ... maths lessons were horrific.' In fact Cockroft (1982: 8), in his government report, concludes that a most 'striking feature' of this study was how maths could induce feelings of anxiety, fear, helplessness and guilt.

Many of us will have intelligent friends and colleagues who fear mathematics to this day; one particular friend describes lining up outside the classroom before the start of the lesson, feeling sick and frozen with fear. It is little wonder then that this results in adults who are quick to denounce their mathematical ability, perhaps partly as a defence mechanism, safeguarding them from perceived future stress and humiliation.

Anxiety is by no means the only negative attitude expressed. Research by Nardi and Stewart (2003) also suggests five other reoccurring attitudinal themes: maths is tedious; isolating; rote; elitist; and depersonalised (T.I.R.E.D), and that many had already labelled themselves at a 'disturbingly young age' as able or unable to do it.

Negative attitudes, when analysed, are often associated with poor pedagogy. Bad practices which include 'being put on the spot' and feeling humiliated in front of others, or the notion that maths is all about speed, 'if you're not fast, you're not good'. Under this pressure all too often we focus more on the 'ticking clock' than the question in hand. Buxton's research (1985) confirms this, demonstrating an effect of near paralysis of rational thinking.

Strangely, some students who find this aspect so stressful themselves when completing 'skills tests' find it difficult to empathise with children in their class, often providing the same stressful environment. We do of course concede that being able to rapidly recall certain facts is extremely valuable; however, it is crucial that mathematics is seen to be a thoughtful, creative and investigative subject, where there can be *more* than 'one right answer' and time to reflect is valued. It is unlikely that you would be asked to write the opening line to a poem in ten seconds!

Another influential factor appears to be the perceived relevance of mathematics. Karp *et al.* (1998) describes a poster that hung on a wall in a dorm, 'Have no fear ... in real life there is no algebra!' Many people cannot see the value of 'school maths' or its relevance in the real world. Skemp (1989) associates this with instrumental learning, which is memorised but not understood. Knowing rules and facts can of course be very useful, but it needs to be embedded in a rich layer of understanding. Facts for facts' sake are pretty useless, and lead to frustrations and failure when they cannot be applied in changing circumstances. Indeed, many of you will have a maths GSCE, but could you solve a simultaneous equation now? And more importantly could you *pose* one, relating it to real life? A truly numerate person is not simply a 'problem solver' but also a 'problem poser'.

Many of the brave among us have asked teachers for explanations but may have been told to simply 'learn it'! Could this perhaps be down to the fact that those very teachers were themselves taught mathematics instrumentally? Perhaps their skills lie in remembering procedures rather than understanding real-life application. Like Suggate (2010: 6), we feel it is likely that 'mathematics which cannot be used or applied in a range of practical circumstances is mathematics which is not understood' or seen as relevant. Consider for a moment quadratic equations: were you introduced to these through Babylonian taxes, area and aesthetic architectural curves and arches, or through formulas alone?

The latter approach may well lead to children saying that mathematics has no relevance in their lives. However, in reality they often engage in numerate behaviour without even realising it. Take for example Figure 2.1: my 14-year-old son's notice board! He also expresses just such views about irrelevance; however, you can see how he happily chooses to record his PlayStation progress to date! Perhaps these are missed opportunities for teachers to build upon, and provide insight into ways we could weld links between 'school' maths and 'home' maths.

Yes, the application of mathematics surrounds us. Standing on a train platform, I glance around and quickly see 'half price; 10% off; £20 for 300 minutes; carriage 3 of 5; maps of underground; digital clocks and train timetables' to name a very few. Then I look further to see arrays on the ceiling, windows translating down the carriages and transformations all around me. Yet do others see this mathematical world? Turner and McCullough (2004: 137) feel making connections is at the heart of creating a love for this subject and understanding its relevance, yet a MaST trainee reported 'we had a cross-curricular week in my school – none of the staff chose to do anything mathematical'.

Classroom practices have, on the whole, progressed somewhat over recent decades, but negative attitudes persist and there is still much room for improvement. Haylock (2010: 7) asks us, as professionals, to reflect: 'Those of us who teach mathematics must pause and wonder what it is that we do to children' which produces adults with such negativity towards the subject.

Reflective task

Do you recognise any of these feelings when you consider your own experiences of learning mathematics at school?

If so, why do you think they occurred for you; were any of these factors influential?

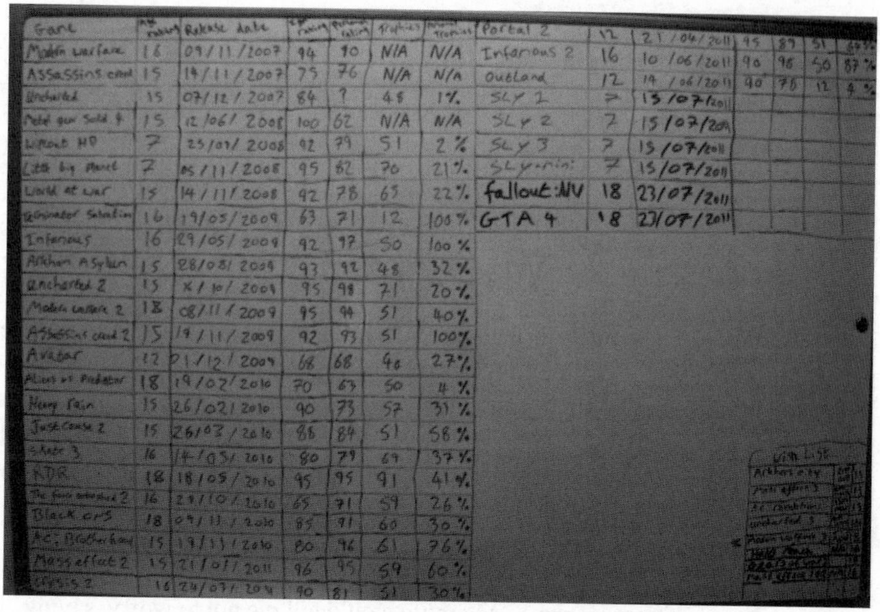

■ **Figure 2.1** A photograph of my son's notice board in his bedroom

Parental influence over developing attitudes

Parental attitudes may also be highly significant in developing both the ability and attitudes of their own children. In his review, Williams (2008) clearly states that parents' attitudes have a significant impact on their children's numeracy skills. Parents are usually a constant and central element in the daily lives of their children and as such will have a direct impact on their educational outcomes. Winter *et al.* (2009) reiterates this, clearly identifying that school is certainly not the only place that learning happens.

Pound (2008) believes that as babies we learn through facial expressions, gestures and body language, resulting in an increased understanding of the thoughts and views of others. From the adults that are most important to them, they learn what to think about the world around them. This has strong implications for adults supporting the mathematical development of their offspring and implies that the extent of this development will be highly dependent on the parents' own attitudes and ability, and will therefore result in positive outcomes for some, but negative outcomes for others.

The work of Young-Loveridge (1989), cited in Gifford (2005), supports this, identifying a link between families who raise the profile of mathematics in their daily routines and children who were 'young experts'. Gifford (2005) finds that positive encouragement leads to children saying *they* are good at maths and demonstrating confidence. Skemp (1989) finds that this confidence leads to a self-fulfilling prophecy – succeeding because you think you can! These parents realise their *own* potential in affecting outcomes, as stated by Desforges (2003). In addition, their own confidence has a positive effect on the child's perceptions and self-image as a learner.

Unfortunately the reverse will also be true; children can be disadvantaged by parental attitudes. Pound (2008) suggests that parents who lack confidence will avoid exploring mathematics in the real world with their children. Research by Young-Loveridge (1989) goes further, identifying a clear link between children with little experience of mathematics and mothers who hated it. But the implications for these children reaches much further than just a 'lack of experience with number'; Skemp (1989) believes that this low status at home and parents' own fear, communicated unwittingly, can go on to cause stress in the young. 'A parent expressing such sentiments can hardly be conducive to a learning environment at home in which mathematics is seen by children as an essential and rewarding part of their everyday lives' (Williams 2008: 3). This may well go on to produce negative attitudes in childhood which could be difficult to change.

Consequently, children's failure is often seen by parents as 'to be expected' and becomes self-perpetuating: 'My mum would tell me not to worry, saying "it's alright, we're all hopeless at maths!"' (Haylock 2010: 9). Clearly there is a perceived link between the outcomes of parents and their offspring; parents who did not succeed themselves often expect the same of their children. Karp *et al.* (1998) describes parents admitting that their children had inherited their own dislike for the subject and had consequently struggled.

Is it possible then that all this creates a vicious circle which may well prove difficult to break? Children who have less experience of numbers when they start school begin behind their peers; they struggle to make up ground and do less well; parents confirm that this is to be expected, as they couldn't do it either; children believe that this is the best outcome they can expect and so lose interest or feel negative. Perhaps this is too contrived, but for some children it does appear to have credence.

Of course the truth is that most parents are desperate to help their children succeed, and do not realise the harm caused by avoiding mathematical experiences or by negative remarks. Donaldson (2002: 69) confirms this, stating 'a large majority of parents actively wish to support their children's learning of mathematics' but this is the subject likely to cause the most anxiety; in addition to previous negative experiences which hold them back, they are now also concerned about 'doing it the wrong way'.

This is a commonly identified issue, confirmed even in popular fiction. Ben Elton (2009) in *Meltdown* describes parental attitudes in the playground. They complain that they hate maths and how methods have changed and they cannot understand them! Added to this, Winter *et al.* (2009) discovers those who feel less able to help can find it quite scary that their children know more than they do. This brings forth another scenario: parents already lacking confidence due to past experiences try to support their children but are told 'that is not how we do it, you don't understand' thus perpetuating parents' own feelings of inadequacy and negativity. This is a real concern, as Fraser and Honeyford (2000) identify, because attitudes and confidence play a huge part in parental effectiveness.

Reflective task

How do you involve parents in your school?

Do they fully understand what their children are doing so that they can provide valuable support?

EXPLORING THE DIFFICULTIES EXPERIENCED BY SOME OF OUR PRIMARY SCHOOL TEACHERS

Our primary school teachers are intelligent, in the top 30 per cent nationally, so it is easy to assume that they would not have negative attitudes or issues with mathematics. Unfortunately this is not the case. Our teachers are also the product of the many influences we have explored thus far, and consequently similar attitudes prevail among some of them. Suggate *et al.* (2010: 2) tell us that 'mathematics has a troubled place in the emotions of many highly intelligent learners' who are 'mentally scarred by past experiences'. In fact, Haylock (2010) suggests that for those with academic qualifications there is the added feeling of guilt that they 'ought' to understand more. Lewis (1996: 11) suggests that for these teachers 'teaching mathematics can be rather like having to teach visitors to a wildlife park all about snakes, when we have a phobia of them ourselves'.

This is a real issue because, as Cockburn (1999) identifies, teachers who dislike maths will find it difficult to be enthusiastic about teaching it. Fox and Surtees (2010) recognise that such enthusiasm is essential and infectious and a key way in which we can really improve attitudes, whereas 'teacher anxiety' has a counter effect, as these anxieties 'can often be passed on to the children they teach', thus perpetuating the cycle of negativity (Haylock 2010: 5). Research by Askew *et al.* (1997) agrees that 'teachers' own negative attitudes to mathematics' can have a significant influence upon children.

For many of these teachers the problem stems from both a lack of confidence due to poor conceptual understanding, and their own negative experiences of learning mathematics. The Royal Society (2010: 5) suggests that inadequate conceptual understanding 'may well be responsible for the progressive disaffection measured in attitudinal research'. Where understanding is limited and connections cannot be made, teachers may see it as pointless and tedious, and perpetuate this by teaching it in this way. Maxwell (2001) suggests that these teachers often grab text books to survive, which is unlikely to produce children who see maths as dynamic or creative; a worksheet-led culture is not conducive to this. Tucker (2005) describes seeing a child with a non-engaging worksheet – bored and miserable. What had been achieved, other than a feeling of failure?

However, Fraser and Honeyford (2000) find evidence that some teachers recognise their issues and become determined not to repeat this pattern. Askew *et al.* (1997: 80) confirmed this when interviewing teachers, 'I would never say to a child "oh aren't you stupid" or "what a silly way to do that" ... because I know what it can feel like.' These teachers may also plan more thoroughly to support their weaknesses, although it could be argued that they would be in a weaker position to deal with questions and misconceptions which could disadvantage their children.

Subject knowledge itself can also be a tricky issue here. You may consider that those with higher-level maths qualification would be excellent teachers; however, much research, including Askew *et al.* (1997), concludes that there is no such correlation. In fact many of these teachers themselves show significant gaps in their conceptual understanding, having been taught mathematics as a set of rules to be memorised and a recipe to be followed. Williams (2008) reiterates that it would be a mistake to equate A-level and good teaching. Recently a trainee teacher with A-level maths revealed 'I never saw the connections; I know 2 cubed is $2 \times 2 \times 2$ but I never saw it as an actual cube.'

Suggate (2010) goes further, stating that if you have been taught in this way, you may be quite unaware of your lack of relational understanding. This could lead to overconfident, procedural teaching which lacks models and images and cannot be accessed by the learner. These teachers may find it difficult to understand why some children cannot remember it, leading to frustration – fuelled by their inability to model it in other ways. Cockburn (1999) concurs, arguing that they may well have an inability to relate to the difficulties of others because they themselves were good at rote learning. As emphasised by the DfES (2004), in order to be a good teacher of mathematics it is important to have the ability to transform your subject knowledge so that others can learn from it.

We can see then that negativity may come in a number of guises, and as Suggate *et al.* (2010) recognise, this is not a desirable state of mind for any teacher who will be playing a significant part in shaping the attitudes of children. A report by the General Teaching Council (GTC) (2010: 23) states that children are 'expert at detecting teacher mood, respect and interest' and Turner and McCullough (2004: 137) tell teachers 'you need ... to be a positive role model'.

The rest of this book aims to identify how you can make a difference. Let us now consider some ways in which a MaST can influence change.

REFLECTING ON THE WAY FORWARD AND HOW YOU CAN PLAY A PART IN AFFECTING CHANGE

A MaST trainee recently reported that when she introduced 'a maths and science week' to staff, one teacher exclaimed 'Oh no ...what have we done to deserve that!' So is change even possible?

NCETM (2010b) strongly suggest that it is possible to change attitudes. They cite previous examples of wholesale change in attitudes relating to gender and race in our society which have taken place in recent years: 'An excellent example of cultural change is the way in which we no longer find acceptable certain forms of racist discourse.' It is certainly true that the media played a part in this, but of equal importance was education. Education is about forming views, and teachers certainly influence the next generation. This is where you come in.

You need to develop a confident and enthusiastic workforce within your school, and a good place to start is by unpicking past experiences and allowing teachers to expose and explore the roots of any attitudinal issues they may have. Research by Zan and Di Martino (2007) presents a way to analyse attitudes, overcome them and put forward a model for change. They encourage participants to analyse their attitudes using three types of personal descriptors:

- ■ The first of these is predominately emotional – 'I like/dislike mathematics'.
- ■ The second is about perceived success at the subject – 'I can/can't do this'.
- ■ The third is internalised understanding of the nature of mathematics and a personal definition – 'mathematics is …'.

They find that these are clearly inter-related in forming attitudes. This model, based on self-reflection, could be a useful one to provide a real in-depth understanding and to begin to make changes (see Figure 2.2).

The NCETM also puts forward a similar model for promoting change. Its activities include:

- ■ exploring personal journeys to date
- ■ considering feelings about maths (including learned habits of emotional association)
- ■ personally defining mathematics
- ■ reflecting and focusing upon 'where next?'

You may well use such material to raise staff awareness and help leave emotional baggage behind. Cotton (2010: 3) also identifies this 'need to make a break with past experiences' so we can move forward.

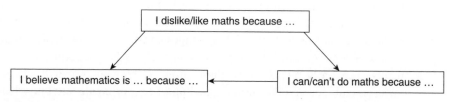

■ **Figure 2.2** A model to promote discussion and support a move towards changing attitudes. Adapted from a diagram by Zan and Di Martino (2007)

Indeed, Skemp (1989) believes reflecting on personal experiences allows us to redesign the negatives to how they should have been. This is crucial for teachers, as it may mean that their pupils are less likely to perpetuate the same negative attitudes. Bottle (2005) identifies that teachers modelling positive views act as advocates and NCETM place a real emphasis on the fact that teachers have 'an individual impact on the attitudes they encounter in their daily lives' and can help or hinder progress.

Often when teachers are made explicitly aware of these issues, they seek change themselves, perhaps never having reflected upon such implications before. An example of this can be taken from a local conference which examined the overall damage caused by British attitudes; one attendee said 'I often say I am no good at maths, and so do my friends. We do it without even thinking ... now things will change!' Richards (1982), cited in Fraser and Honeyford (2000: 77), confirms the importance of such an approach, saying 'it is unfortunate that we sometimes accept the common "I just can't do mathematics" excuse'. We need to sensitively challenge such thinking when we meet it.

It is also crucial to move away from guilt or blame when making a fresh start and to create an environment where staff feel able to discuss concerns and gaps in knowledge without being judged. Lewis (1996: 176) suggests that self-reproach can lead to despondency which will infect the atmosphere of learning. We need to 'relax' more about mathematics and not be too hard on ourselves. The best thing you can demonstrate is a 'willingness to learn yourself, to work with colleagues and to ask the really obvious questions which others may not have the confidence to raise' (Ma 1999: 296).

In fact one of the reasons why we, as authors, feel that our consortium has been successful in its delivery of the MaST programme is the way we work together as a team; all of us willing to say 'can you explain that again' or retort 'well, I never knew that'; no one scared to be exposed and everyone with a thirst for enquiry and a love of all things mathematical. There is always so much more to learn – the more you discover, the more this becomes apparent. Skemp (1989) agrees that creating a relaxed atmosphere, where mistakes are seen as learning opportunities and everyone contributes, provides valuable emotional support. Staff that experience this are more likely to replicate it in their classrooms.

So once you have confronted the past and created a supportive environment, perhaps a sense of fun can improve attitudes further. A paper by Maxwell (2001: 30), about encouraging positive learning dispositions, finds that a key element is the need to generate enjoyment. Koshy (1999: 14) states that 'we all know that we learn better if we enjoy what we are learning' and almost a decade on Ofsted (2008) confirms the importance of enjoyment to promote learning. But do we see mathematics as 'fun'? Pound (2008) suggests that we readily engage in playfulness in most aspects of child development but rarely is this done in relation to mathematics. The Early Years Curriculum Group (1993) notes that teachers have the power to embrace and encourage a feeling of fun, or create an atmosphere of 'dull drudgery'. Remember the words of George Bernard Shaw: 'To educate, you must first entertain.'

It would be useful to encourage colleagues to consider what actually motivates *them* to learn, alongside imagining themselves as 'a child' in their own classroom; would they want to be there? Recently, when discussing the importance of moving away from the 'one hand one answer' approach, a MaST trainee shared her 'pulling names from a pot' idea; however, when it was then suggested by the tutor that the same method was used with the group, the trainee quickly realised how anxious that made her feel – empathy is important if you want to create a positive and safe environment.

Many books provide information about leading mathematics or coordinating it within a school. Rarely do they focus upon raising positive attitudes; we strongly believe they should. Williams (2008: 62) concurs, stating that in schools 'too little attention is paid to building good attitudes to mathematics'. NCETM sees the long-term vision for the MaST as 'making the subject more attractive to children, colleagues and parents'. It describes specialist teachers as 'local hubs of influence', leading to 'more positive attitudes, higher expectations and higher standards in mathematics for all'.

Specialist teachers are *already* making a difference. An example of this comes from a MaST, mentoring a nervous NQT. Afterwards the NQT said 'I can't wait to teach this now … I'm really excited about it.' Cotton (2010: 210) believes that promoting this 'can do attitude … can really start to overcome the fear of mathematics', and once this is in place teachers will be open to further developing their subject knowledge and pedagogy and real progress will be made.

CONCLUSIONS

'Learners, teachers, parents, academics, business leaders, politicians all say there is a serious problem with mathematics education, so it must be true' (Williams and Ryan 2007: 1). Such an extensive problem will need a strategic long-term solution, designed to counter these stereotypical views of both mathematics and mathematicians.

We *all* need to be part of this. The media and politicians need to tackle this at a national level, providing positive images and role models in our daily lives – more Hermione Grangers! Alongside this we will need teachers and parents who can create positive experiences for the next generation of adults. This dynamic, multifaceted approach could have a significant impact, as has been seen in the past in terms of sexuality, race and gender.

Carol Vorderman (*Guardian* 2008) strongly believes that 'our children are not stupid; our children are not inherently inadequate; our children are not born hating maths, we just manage to convince them that they should!' In the same article, the Minister for Schools in 2008, Andrew Adonis, said 'we all have our part to play in reversing the "can't do attitude" – carers, childminders, parents and teachers – we *all* need to change attitudes' (ibid.).

So now you need to ask yourself whether you too are passionate about this … and up for a challenge!

Reflective task

During a casual staff room conversation a member of staff declares 'I really don't like maths … I have always hated teaching it.'

Now you have read this chapter would you respond any differently?

FURTHER READING

Guardian (1999) *Teachers Too Ashamed to Admit Inability in Maths*. 2 September.

CHAPTER 3

DEEP SUBJECT KNOWLEDGE

INTRODUCTION

This chapter aims to explore the nature of deep subject knowledge and to challenge and support you in reviewing your own mathematical understanding by:

1   considering some theories and ideas about teacher knowledge generally, and in primary mathematics in particular. This will help to define what subject knowledge is and underpin the rest of the chapter.

2   exploring some of the features of effective subject knowledge which have already been identified in the literature. These features build up a picture of deep subject knowledge and will challenge you to analyse your own knowledge. These features include:

a   making mathematical connections

b   tracing mathematical progression

c   identifying key mathematical ideas

d   using and applying mathematics

3   concluding with some key questions aimed to challenge your subject knowledge.

The *Independent Review of Mathematics in Primary Schools and Early Years Settings* (Williams 2008: 7) argued that teachers should draw on deep subject knowledge to teach mathematics effectively, as well as pedagogical knowledge: 'The main thrust of this review, therefore, is that a *combination* of deep subject knowledge and pedagogical skill is required to promote effective learning.' One of Williams' ten key recommendations was that 'there should be at least one Mathematics Specialist in each primary school with deep subject knowledge in mathematics' (2008: 3). Part of the role of the mathematics specialist teacher is to support the subject knowledge of their colleagues.

As you take on the role of specialist teacher, you will need to review your subject knowledge. Deep subject knowledge should enable you to support learning across your school, perhaps from a nursery setting to Year 6. You may well have an in-depth subject knowledge of the mathematics in the curriculum for particular year groups where you have much experience of teaching, but not of other year groups. In this chapter we will consider what sort of mathematical knowledge you need to have to support children's learning in the whole of the primary range.

Reflective task

Your mathematical subject knowledge will have been judged as secure as you were awarded Qualified Teaching Status. Consider the subject knowledge you use as you draw up a yearly plan for a new class, plan for learning through a topic or unit of work, or use day-to-day assessment to prepare and teach a lesson. What mathematical knowledge do you need? Has your subject knowledge changed since qualifying?

TEACHER KNOWLEDGE

Teachers develop and draw on a particular type of knowledge to teach children. Sometimes it is difficult to pinpoint exactly the knowledge teachers need to teach well.

Shulman (1986, 1987) was one of the first writers to try to describe teachers' knowledge. He claimed that teachers' knowledge is different from knowledge which other people have. He identified seven domains of categories of teacher knowledge, two of which are particularly relevant to this book. He called subject matter content knowledge 'the amount and organisation of knowledge per se in the mind of the teacher' (1986: 9). In our case, this would be knowledge of the subject of mathematics. He also identified a further category as pedagogical content knowledge. This category he described as comprising the 'useful forms of representation …, powerful analogies, illustrations, examples, explanations, demonstrations' (1986: 9) which can be used to teach the subject to others. This category will be discussed in depth in the following chapter.

Shulman's work has been discussed in depth since the 1980s. It offers a useful base to begin to think about teachers' knowledge. However, the work has been critiqued as assuming a technical model of teaching and learning (Aubrey 1997; Poulson 2001). Shulman seems to suggest that teachers transform their subject matter content knowledge and transmit this to children. Teaching is complex, and does not follow a linear model where knowledge is acquired, stored and transmitted to others.

Teachers' knowledge of subject content seems to be connected to the classroom. When you reflect on your development as a teacher, much of your mathematical knowledge may well have been learned as you taught an area of mathematics or prepared to teach it. Do you think there is a clear distinction between Shulman's categories of subject matter content knowledge and pedagogical content knowledge? Teachers' knowledge and understanding of the mathematics they teach is clearly linked to their understanding and experiences of children's learning. For example, when you prepare to teach a certain area of mathematics you probably draw on mathematical knowledge but also your memories of what has been successful before in similar teaching, the aspects you find children generally struggle with and your assessment of the children in your present class. Teachers develop mathematical and teaching knowledge together. However, for the purposes of this book, subject knowledge and pedagogical knowledge will be explored separately in this and the following chapter, while recognising that the two are intertwined. This is to enable us to consider them in depth.

For the purposes of this chapter and the whole book, the term subject knowledge will be used rather than Shulman's subject matter content knowledge. It is defined as teachers' knowledge which is mathematical. It develops with respect to teaching and learning, but it is mathematical knowledge. For example, it might be the mathematical knowledge needed to create problems for children to work on, to explain mathematical vocabulary, differentiate tasks, or assess children's rapid recall of number facts. Ball *et al.* (2008) termed this type of teacher knowledge as pure specialised knowledge. This is knowledge which is pure in that it is mathematical and not connected to particular learners, and specialised in that it is not found in any other person other than a teacher, or used in any other setting. Do you agree with this? Is your mathematical knowledge as a teacher different from the sort of knowledge of someone in any other profession who draws on the same areas of mathematics?

The focus of this chapter then is on an analysis of the mathematical knowledge you need to be a specialist teacher, as well as an effective classroom teacher of mathematics. There are two things here to consider:

■ Exactly what mathematics do teachers need to have knowledge of?
■ How should teachers understand this mathematics?

Consider the first question. What mathematics do you need to understand as a primary teacher? You would probably agree that you need an accurate understanding of the mathematical ideas and vocabulary represented in the curriculum for the ages of the children you teach, and to be able to answer without any difficulty any questions and problems set for this age range. Would you also include the mathematics curriculum for the key stage above and below? For example, would you want to know and understand the mathematics that children will learn in Year 7? Would you extend this to the end of Key Stage 3, or beyond? Where does your knowledge need to extend to? Do you need to understand learning which usually takes place before children start school? Later in this chapter, the need to understand the mathematics covered in previous and future learning of children will be discussed.

In response to the second question, how teachers understand this mathematics is more difficult to define and quantify. It is the quality of teachers' understanding of primary mathematics which makes their subject knowledge deep. In the rest of this chapter we will explore the features of deep subject knowledge. Before these features are identified, two key pieces of work will be considered.

First, we will consider the research of Ma (1999). She used interviews to investigate the structure of teachers' mathematical knowledge rather than their formal qualification. The interviews probed teachers' understanding of teaching scenarios. For example, they were asked to provide real-life contexts for division by fractions. Her findings led Ma to define a profound understanding of mathematics as one which is deep in that it is connected with conceptually powerful ideas of mathematics and broad in that it is connected to other topics and ideas. This chapter will refer to Ma's work in the following discussion of key features of deep subject knowledge in primary mathematics.

A second key work is based on research aiming to investigate and describe the types of knowledge needed by primary teachers as they teach mathematics. The work of Rowland *et al.* (2009) is written to particularly aid student teachers but also supports all teachers in developing their primary mathematics teaching. They provide a very useful way of categorising teachers' knowledge, called the knowledge quartet. These four domains of knowledge are described as:

1   *Foundation*. This category includes teachers' mathematical subject knowledge, for example their knowledge of vocabulary or properties of numbers. It also includes their theoretical knowledge of teaching and learning, and their beliefs and values about mathematics.

2   *Transformation*. This is teachers' knowledge of how to present and explain mathematical ideas to children. It is evident in teachers' planning and teaching, and includes their choice of examples, resources, representations and the way teachers demonstrate mathematics themselves in their teaching.

3   *Connection*. This category is the knowledge that teachers have of mathematical connections and how to support progress in children's learning. Teachers draw on this knowledge as they plan a sequence of activities, lessons or topics, moving from simple to more complex ideas. It requires teachers to know what is appropriate for children and to plan for the next steps. It is evident in planning and teaching across a short activity, a lesson or a series of lessons.

4   *Contingency*. This type of knowledge is evident only in teaching. It involves teachers' reactions to events they have not anticipated; their ability to think on their feet. It includes responses to children's unexpected ideas and comments, and a willingness to change their plans.

The knowledge quartet provides an enlightening tool for analysing teacher knowledge. It encompasses more than teachers' mathematical knowledge and therefore provides an underpinning basis for the exploration in this book of both subject and pedagogical knowledge. Overt mathematical knowledge is represented specifically in the foundation category of the quartet, but also underpins other categories. For example, mathematical knowledge is an aspect of the connection and contingency categories. Teachers draw on mathematical knowledge to plan tasks and to respond to children's mathematical questions and comments. In fact, Rowland *et al.*

(2009) state that the other three dimensions of the quartet rest on the foundation category. It can be assumed that the knowledge quartet represents the sort of knowledge that all teachers of mathematics should draw upon, and therefore to be considered as deep, the subject and pedagogical knowledge of specialist teachers should be particularly well developed in each of the four categories. Therefore, the work of Rowland *et al.* will be drawn on throughout this chapter, to challenge your own mathematical understanding and illuminate ideas of deep subject knowledge.

Features of deep subject knowledge

This section of the chapter aims to identify and discuss key features the current literature has used to describe subject knowledge for mathematics teaching, in order to explore what might be deep subject knowledge. These ideas might challenge your own existing subject knowledge. Remember that as a specialist teacher, you need to develop a deep knowledge of the mathematics across the primary curriculum, not just for the specific year groups you usually teach.

Connected mathematical knowledge

First we will consider the argument that the sort of subject knowledge teachers need, and the sort of understanding they should promote in children, can be described as connected. Therefore, deep subject knowledge in teachers should include a strong element of connectedness.

Reflective task

What does this mean for you? Consider your last mathematics lesson. Did you find yourself making connections to:

a previous lesson and your assessment of children's learning in it?

a topic covered in another area of the curriculum?

children's current interests? A new film, a local shop, playground, something in the school or grounds?

a previous mathematical topic where you might have discussed a similar idea, or the same idea in another form?

Did you cover one idea in a variety of ways? It may have been expressed in different language, or recorded in more than one way, or you may have considered the same idea in different contexts.

Do you aim to make connections with children in your mathematics lessons? Can you say why?

During 2008, two influential documents by Williams and Ofsted called for teachers to teach children to understand mathematics. What does understanding mathematics mean and are there different ways of understanding it? When we look at how some writers have tried to define mathematical understanding, we see that they describe it as connected. For example, writers now often still make use of terms first introduced by Skemp (1989) to discuss the nature of mathematical understanding.

Skemp (1989) defined two types of understanding, relational understanding and instrumental understanding, using the analogy of walking around a city. Relational understanding can be thought of as similar to walking around a city one is familiar with, where it is possible to take a number of routes between any two places. The walker can make the best choice about which route is most appropriate to take. The city is understood as a network of connections. Instrumental understanding may be thought of as following a set of rules or instructions to navigate an unfamiliar city where the walker may know only one or two routes between certain places and is unable to deviate from these routes. A learner who draws on relational understanding of, say, subtraction is able to call on a number of methods to solve particular problems and justify the method they use. A learner with instrumental knowledge may have a successful method of solving certain problems, but has little flexibility to tackle anything different.

Therefore, teaching which promotes children's understanding seems to have been best described as teaching which helps children to make connections. This idea is backed by research undertaken by Askew *et al.* (1997) which aimed to identify the characteristics of effective teachers of numeracy. It suggested that highly effective teachers believed that being numerate requires a rich network of connections between mathematical ideas, allowing children to choose effective and efficient strategies. Effective teachers tend to connect ideas in different and the same area of mathematics using language, symbols and diagrams. Some but not all of the less effective teachers had compartmentalised knowledge.

Reflective task

Is your understanding of mathematics connected and relational? Reflect on your ability to:

take a mathematical idea and make connections to resources, stories, themes, real and imaginative contexts;

take a resource, story, theme or a real or imaginative context and identify the mathematical ideas which could be connected to it;

explore one idea with a variety of language, recordings and in a range of contexts.

A connected knowledge of mathematics can be argued as essential for teachers because it reflects the structure of mathematics itself. Mathematics is a connected body of knowledge. Counting underlies the four number operations. Addition is the inverse of subtraction, multiplication can be thought of as repeated addition. Mathematics has a certain regularity based on patterns and generalisations which provides its elegance. It seems therefore that mathematics itself has a connected structure. If children learn mathematics by making sense of a number of connections within mathematics, then teachers themselves need to understand and make these connections. Would you agree with this idea?

If deep subject knowledge of mathematics is connected in nature, then this can be thought of in two ways. Teachers need to make hierarchical connections to support progression in children's learning. This will be discussed in depth in the next section. They also need to recognise equivalent forms of mathematical ideas and make sideways connections.

Reflective task

How many ways can you think of to present the mathematical idea of ¾ or 2 + 3 = 5 to children?

Gray and Tall (2007) discuss compression as a key feature of mathematics. Mathematics compresses a number of situations, problems and questions into a simple model such as 2 + 3 = 5. It notates ideas in a short, abbreviated way. This is its strength. The art of a mathematics teacher is to do the opposite, to expand 2 + 3 = 5 into its various forms for children to develop a full understanding of its meaning (Davis and Simmt 2006). In mathematics there are many examples of equivalent ideas expressed in different forms. For example, 2 + 4 is the same as 6 or 10 − 4, and 12 × 7 is the same as (10 × 7) + (2 × 7). ACME (2008) suggests that equivalence is one of the four big ideas of the primary curriculum. The ability to make valid connections between representations seems to be significant. The research by Ma (1999) found that teachers with what she termed profound understanding were able to make and discuss specific links, for example between manipulatives and mathematical ideas, or between standard and non-standard methods. This is also a feature of the connection category of the knowledge quartet (Rowland *et al.* 2009).

Teachers' subject knowledge therefore needs to support them in presenting the same idea in various representations and connecting linked ideas. Wilson *et al.* (1987) discussed a teacher who felt he needed to know mathematics in 150 ways in order to teach it. It may also be necessary to know mathematics wrongly 150 ways in order to analyse children's errors to assess their learning. However, knowledge of parallel ideas and sideways connections may not be sufficient. For example, if children do not understand an idea in mathematics, it may not be effective simply to try another approach and continue to do so in an ad hoc manner. Teachers' mathematical knowledge can support them in identifying what the child does understand and to make a corresponding link. They can also make connections to children's changing interests, contexts and learning needs. Teaching mathematics can be described as dynamic in responding to the immediate needs of the learners (Ainley and Luntley 2005; Poulson 2001). Deep subject knowledge is about choosing the most effective connection to make.

The ability to draw connections between mathematical ideas and representations of the same idea therefore appears to be an important part of a definition of deep subject knowledge. This includes being aware of multiple equivalent ideas or representations of the same idea, and the ability to reason and choose between them. Some hierarchical connections are more important than others because they support progression in children's learning. This will be discussed in the next key theme.

Understanding mathematical progression

In this section we will discuss the role of specialist teachers in understanding where children's learning will develop to, and how it has already progressed. Mathematics can be seen as a hierarchical subject in some senses. Children usually learn about small numbers before they learn about large numbers. They tend to draw on their knowledge of number facts to ten when they solve problems with numbers up to 100. However, children's learning is often not as linear and predictable as this; young children, for example, can be interested in very large numbers.

An analysis of the way in which mathematical ideas build on each other in a hierarchical way can support teachers in planning a series of experiences for children. It can also aid them in the process of assessment for learning, planning to extend children's understanding or analysing errors. This is recognised in Rowland et al.'s (2009) category of connection.

First, an understanding of progression implies that teachers can analyse children's previous learning. Ma (1999) asked teachers to list the prior knowledge children need to learn a particular mathematical idea, calling this a knowledge package. Teachers often consider a knowledge package when they plan a topic or week's work in mathematics. For example, if the key idea to be covered over a week is addition of three-digit numbers, teachers will consider what prior knowledge needs to be in place. Ma found that some teachers were able to articulate these packages with clarity and detail. The argument here is that deep mathematical understanding allows you to identify past learning to underpin new learning.

An understanding of previous learning can help teachers to analyse when progress does not take place. All teachers need to be able to use children's errors and misconceptions as a form of assessment for learning. This enables teachers to trace learning back, analyse errors and identify and tackle misconceptions. As a specialist teacher you can have an overview of errors across the primary phase and explore how and why they might occur.

Reflective task

What prior knowledge would you want to cover before teaching children to add three-digit numbers? What is in the knowledge package?

A primary mathematics specialist teacher also calls on the deep subject knowledge which relates to future learning. This means understanding progression in children's learning from the Early Years into Key Stage 3. This can support you in the ability to trace mathematical ideas through the curriculum to support possible lines of progression and state long-term goals (Ma 1999; Rowland *et al.* 2009 connection aspect of the knowledge quartet). Otherwise, it is possible to limit future learning. For example, when first introducing the equals sign to young children, teachers' use of the word 'makes' to explain its meaning in a number sentence such as $2 + 3 = 5$ promotes misconceptions which become apparent when the child later tackles problems such as $6 = 2 + ?$. The key meaning of $=$ is 'the same as'. A further example would be the teaching of young children to multiply by ten by adding a zero to the end of the number, a method which does not support the multiplication of decimals by ten later in the curriculum. Specialist teachers can foresee later learning (Ma 1999).

Deep subject knowledge can enable specialist teachers to state the big ideas of mathematics (ACME 2008) and to see learning as moving towards these. Twiselton (2000) found that strategies such as the National Literacy Strategy tend to obscure the rationale for the subject itself, which should provide coherence and cohesion to teaching. Teaching can then become a delivery of fragmented learning objectives, all presented as equally important, with no feel of moving towards a big idea.

The specialist teacher's role in supporting progression in children's learning requires knowledge and understanding of a series of hierarchical connections between ideas. Some connections and ideas can be considered more important than others. This will be discussed in the next section.

Identifying key mathematical ideas

This section will consider how deep subject knowledge includes the ability to identify the key mathematical ideas in a topic, lesson or activity, rather than those on the periphery. For example, consider a teacher who focuses on drawing graphs rather than interpreting them, or who provides examples of word problems only after teaching each of the operations, with little chance to engage children with making decisions about which operations to use. Subject knowledge can support teachers in identifying the key ideas in an area of mathematics.

A key voice in this area has been Ma (1999) in her exploration of the knowledge of teachers with what she termed profound understanding of mathematics. These teachers were able to identify the single mathematical concept underlying topics in the primary curriculum. They discussed these concepts in their simplest mathematical terms, for example the use of the distributive law in multiplication. They were able to identify and discuss basic mathematics ideas which underpin areas of mathematics.

These ideas link to the work of Bruner (1996), who claimed that any subject can be taught to any child in an honest form and then developed through a spiral curriculum. It can be argued therefore that a specialist's deep subject knowledge can allow them to identify and trace the progression of key mathematical ideas. Given a topic or learning objective for any year group, they might identify the particular underlying mathematical idea, and be able to state when this should have first been introduced to children, how it has already developed and how the idea will continue to develop in later stages of the curriculum.

Reflective task

Would you consider counting as a key idea of the mathematics curriculum?

How do children learn to count? When do children begin to count in twos, fives and tens? What sort of counting is suitable for children in Year 6?

Are you aware of when children in your school are taught other key mathematical ideas such as the importance of the whole in fractions, when they are taught to think systematically, when they are introduced to zero, or when they first begin to learn about place value?

Mathematics by its nature lends itself to abstraction. An understanding of mathematics can support teachers in arranging examples which make clear the particular attributes to abstract (Gray and Tall 2007). For example, when children first grasp the meaning of triangle, they need to know that the important attributes are the number of sides and vertices of the shape rather than its colour, size or orientation. Teachers need to provide examples of shapes which help children to recognise these attributes and tackle the misconception, for example, that one side of a triangle must be horizontal. Children who struggle with mathematics may well attend to different, trivial attributes and abstract incorrectly.

Therefore, we have seen that deep mathematical subject knowledge includes the ability to state the key ideas of the primary curriculum, to know where these are introduced to children, and how they progress through the curriculum.

Using and applying mathematics

The term using and applying mathematics describes the part of the primary curriculum which relates to children's investigation and problem solving, or their work as mathematicians, thinking and reasoning mathematically. In this chapter, the term will also refer to the processes of teachers engaging with investigations and problems, undertaking mathematical enquiry which requires them to think mathematically. This is opposed to solving closed problems, where there might be a set procedure to follow. This section will reflect on the argument for teachers as well as children to use and apply mathematics, and therefore the role of the specialist teacher in this.

For example, research by Ma (1999) found that teachers with profound understanding of mathematics were more likely to investigate mathematics than other teachers. They were familiar with procedures for establishing proofs and were more likely to act as mathematicians, Ma claimed. The argument then is that teachers and children need to engage in processes of solving non-routine problems which require mathematical thinking, generating general statements and exploring mathematical arguments in order to understand how these are constructed by mathematicians. This enables them to learn mathematics which is as yet new to them.

This relates to the way the nature of mathematics is presented to children in school. Mathematics can be about investigation or knowing what has been investigated by others. If mathematics is a subject of enquiry, then only by modelling enquiry can teachers present a full picture of mathematics. Subjects should not be packaged or fragmented (ACME 2008), as this does not present them in their full form.

Freudenthal (1991) describes how ready-made mathematics can be presented to children, which conceals the nature of the subject. Teachers should instead guide children in the activity of mathematics. He claims that text books generally present mathematical vocabulary, for example the term parallelogram, as a given. However, the reaching of a definition such as parallelogram is the result of a human activity. Learners need to grasp the true meaning of the term, what it does and does not include, by their own activity. By engaging with shapes which are and are not parallelograms, they learn the definition and the act of defining for themselves. Teachers should therefore present the activity of mathematics, arguably captured by the terms using and applying, to children rather than ready-made mathematics. Teachers' subject knowledge should therefore support them in guiding children's using and applying mathematics. For this to be so, they need to engage themselves in using and applying mathematics.

Often during open-ended tasks, children ask their own questions and follow an unexpected train of thought. Should teachers allow children to follow red herrings in the belief that this will further their understanding? Should they be able to predict red herrings and guide children through the processes of making sense of them? If so, this involves teachers in engaging with problems and grappling with the red herrings themselves.

Do you feel that as a specialist teacher you will want to encourage your colleagues in using and applying mathematics themselves? This would involve you in supporting them in learning mathematics as yet unknown to them, investigating and problem solving, thinking logically, playing with numbers and ideas to abstract and reach generalisations, and constructing arguments and proofs. Could you encourage this kind of approach among your colleagues?

CONCLUSIONS

This chapter has been written to begin to challenge you to analyse your subject knowledge of primary mathematics. In the area of mathematics which you will teach next in your classroom, can you:

■ state the key connecting mathematical ideas which children will have encountered before?

■ trace the children's future learning to what you feel are the big ideas of mathematics?

■ identify the key mathematical ideas you will teach and consider how these ideas are best represented to allow children to understand them?

■ represent and discuss these mathematical ideas in equivalent ways, using resources or imagined and real-life contexts?

■ connect ideas to children's interests and real lives?

■ engage in investigation in this area of mathematics, considering how children will investigate them too?

In this chapter we have identified features of deep subject knowledge. We have discussed making mathematical connections, key mathematical ideas, progression and using and applying mathematics. Chapters 6, 7 and 8 will consider each of these features in the areas of multiplication, time and data handling, allowing you to reflect on what each might mean in your school in the context of a specific area of mathematics. We hope this will help you to gain an overview of the areas of mathematics for your school and help you to raise levels of learning, expectations and enjoyment.

FURTHER READING

Ma, L. (1999) *Knowing and Teaching Elementary Mathematics: Teachers' Understanding of Fundamental Mathematics in China and the United States*. Mahwah, NJ: Lawrence Erlbaum Associates. This book looks in detail at Ma's findings, comparing teachers' knowledge and exploring her ideas of profound understanding of primary mathematics.

Rowland, T., Turner, F., Thwaites, A. and Huckstep, P. (2009) *Developing Primary Mathematics Teaching*. London: Sage. This book identifies knowledge teachers draw on in their teaching of mathematics, the knowledge quartet, and uses it to analyse examples of mathematics teaching.

CHAPTER 4

PEDAGOGICAL KNOWLEDGE

INTRODUCTION

The argument put forward at the start of the previous chapter was that according to Williams (2008: 7) 'a *combination* of deep subject knowledge and pedagogical skill is required to promote effective learning'. This chapter aims to explore ideas about pedagogy and support you in developing your understanding by:

1 reviewing 'deep subject knowledge';
2 considering some theories and ideas about pedagogy generally and in primary mathematics in particular as Schulman (1986, 1987) suggests that there is a difference between 'general pedagogical knowledge' and 'pedagogical content knowledge';
3 exploring some of the features of 'pedagogical content knowledge' in the context of mathematics which have already been identified in the literature. These features include
   a knowledge of learners of mathematics
   b effective task design
   c resources/representations/analogies/demonstrations/explanations/quest-ioning and discussion
4 considering whether pedagogical knowledge can be separated from 'deep subject knowledge'. Ma (1999: xi) argues that 'conception of content is profoundly pedagogical'.

REVIEW OF THE FEATURES OF DEEP SUBJECT KNOWLEDGE

In the previous chapter we identified the following features of 'deep subject knowledge':

a   Mathematical connections
b   Tracing mathematical progression
c   Identifying key mathematical ideas
d   Using and applying mathematics.

Consider the two questions:

1    $32 - 3 =$
2    $32 - 29 =$

In Chapter 3 we established that subject knowledge is more complex than simply knowing that the answer to question 1 is 29 and the answer to question 2 is 3. Instead it requires an understanding of the four key ideas listed above.

Multiple and parallel connections

The two questions are connected to each other, to other aspects of mathematics and to different contexts.

Progression

Learning about subtraction emerges from an understanding of counting and develops to include a range of mental and written strategies from which children make appropriate choices.

Key mathematical ideas

One key idea is that descriptions of subtraction vary. For example, Turner and McCullouch (2004: 38) list four 'calculation structures' for subtraction (partitioning, reduction, comparison and complementary addition) while Barmby *et al.* (2009: 24) identify different addition and subtraction situations (change situations, combine situations, compare situations and equalise situations). What is clear is that subtraction can be described as both 'take away' and 'difference'.

Using and applying mathematics

This term was used in the previous chapter to describe the processes involved when teachers (or children) are engaging with investigations and problems or undertaking mathematical enquiry which requires them to think mathematically.

> **Reflective task**
>
> From the starting points listed above consider the 'deep subject knowledge' a teacher would need to explore these questions with children.

PEDAGOGICAL CONTENT KNOWLEDGE

Having established a definition of 'deep subject knowledge' and exemplified the key features, it is necessary to explore the term pedagogy in the context of mathematics. The *Independent Review of Mathematics in Primary Schools and Early Years Settings* (Williams 2008: 60) considered the question 'What is the most effective pedagogy of mathematics teaching in primary schools and early years settings?' Under this chapter heading Williams (2008: 63) limits his discussion of a definition of pedagogy to the statement that 'the term pedagogy is generally used by researchers and teacher educators to encompass both classroom practice and the teacher's knowledge and beliefs about the subject and the learning and teaching that underpin it'. He warns that 'there is a danger that pedagogy is interpreted as meaning simply "teaching methods"'. The next section will consider the complexity of the term 'pedagogy' in the context of mathematics in particular. A range of possible definitions of pedagogy are considered below.

Shulman (1986: 9) separates general pedagogical knowledge from pedagogical content knowledge. He describes pedagogical content knowledge as a 'second kind of content knowledge, which goes beyond knowledge of subject matter per se to knowledge of subject matter *for teaching*'. He goes on to suggest that:

> Pedagogical content knowledge also includes an understanding of what makes the learning of specific topics easy or difficult; the concepts and preconceptions that students of different ages and backgrounds bring with them to the learning [...] because learners are unlikely to appear before them as blank slates.

Aubrey (1997: 77) uses the term 'pedagogical subject knowledge' which she states 'lies between subject content knowledge on the one hand and pedagogy on the other'. It is this aspect of pedagogy that is of particular interest. The content of this chapter will consider 'pedagogical knowledge' in the context of mathematics.

The descriptions listed above suggest that pedagogical content knowledge includes a 'knowledge of learners'. Aubrey (1997: 77) makes this more explicit when she notes that pedagogical knowledge 'requires an understanding of pupils' existing knowledge, their typical errors and misconceptions'. Ofsted (2008) develop the theme of 'knowledge of learners' by suggesting that one of the essential ingredients of effective mathematics teaching is an understanding of the ways in which children learn mathematics, i.e. pedagogical content knowledge also includes an understanding of how children learn. This theme is also considered by Williams (2008: 65), who states that 'First and foremost, pedagogy must be learner-centred, in the sense that it is responsive to the needs of the particular children being taught.'

While this does provide some insight into the nature of pedagogy, further detail is required in order to identify other features of pedagogical knowledge. Again it is useful to begin the discussion with Shulman (1986: 9):

> Within the category of pedagogical content knowledge I include, for the most regularly taught topics in one's subject area, the most useful forms of representation of those ideas, the most powerful analogies, illustrations, examples, explanations and demonstrations – in a word, the ways of representing and formulating the subject that make it comprehensible to others.

The DfES (2004: 9) draw on Shulman's work and suggest that 'In order to teach mathematics it is necessary not only to have knowledge of the subject matter of mathematics but also the ability to transform such knowledge so that others may learn it.' Rowland *et al.* (2009: 21) also consider the notion of 'transformation' and suggest that 'In mathematics pedagogical content knowledge refers to how teachers transform their own knowledge into a form that makes it accessible to all learners.' They add the notion that 'Pedagogical content knowledge is also concerned with the way in which teachers break down ideas and explain concepts to learners.'

The final theme emerges from the work of Hiebert *et al.* (1997: 30) who suggest that 'one of the most critical responsibilities for the teacher is setting appropriate tasks'. Hiebert *et al.* (1997: 31) also note that the teacher's role in setting tasks is more complex than simply devising individual tasks one after the other. Instead teachers need to select 'sequences of tasks so that over time, students' experiences add up to something important'. This theme is also developed by Rowland *et al.* (2009: 31) under the heading 'connection' which concerns the:

> coherence of planning or teaching across an episode, lesson or series of lessons. [...] In addition to the connectedness of mathematical content in the mind of the teacher and his/her teaching in the classroom, this dimension includes the sequencing of topics of instruction within and between lessons, including the ordering of tasks and exercises.

Analysis of the research cited has therefore led to a clarification of the term 'pedagogical knowledge' and revealed three key ideas for further consideration:

1   knowledge of learners of mathematics
2   effective task design
3   resources/representations/analogies/demonstrations/explanations.

FEATURES OF 'PEDAGOGICAL KNOWLEDGE' IN THE CONTEXT OF MATHEMATICS

This section of the chapter aims to explore these themes in greater depth. The order in which these ideas are explored is not hierarchical.

Knowledge of 'learners of mathematics'

This section will consider the argument that pedagogical content knowledge includes a knowledge of learners of mathematics in further detail. As stated at the start of this chapter, Shulman (1986) included 'knowledge of learners' under the category of generic teacher knowledge. However, Ball *et al.* (2005) see such knowledge as specialist content knowledge as it requires an understanding of the particular subject area. So, for example, in order to find out what young children understand about subtraction a teacher would need to understand the range of subtraction structures in order to devise appropriate probing questions or rich mathematical activities. This line of argument is pursued below.

Aubrey (1997: 155) argues that the development of good teaching for understanding requires corresponding models of good assessment of higher-order understanding and learning. Her research with reception teachers leads her to conclude that if pedagogical practice is to be enhanced, teachers need to be aware of the mathematical understandings and strategies which young learners bring to school (i.e. the mathematical content) and develop effective approaches for accessing this.

The labelling of approaches to assessing or accessing pupil knowledge and understanding has been the subject of much discussion. The terms 'formative' and 'summative' assessment suggests two discrete approaches to assessment which can be broadly defined as 'assessment for learning' and 'assessment of learning'. Typically AfL or formative assessment describes the process of gathering information about pupils on a day-to-day basis which would then be used to inform short-term planning. Summative assessment describes the process of gathering data about pupils' performance at particular times of the year. It can be used to inform parents, subsequent teachers and the school management team of pupil progress. However, there is potential for summative assessments to be used formatively; if, for example, children are asked to explain the procedures they used to complete a test question or if small groups of children are asked to explore a range of answers to a given problem in a test and decide which one is correct. A range of formative assessments could also be gathered over a period of time and used to make a summative judgement of pupil progress over a period of time. Therefore the differences between these apparent dichotomies may not be as clear-cut as they first appear. What is clear is that whether a formative or a summative approach is taken to assessment learning can only be enhanced if the outcomes of the assessment are used to change subsequent learning activity. Again this indicates a need for subject-specific knowledge of progression.

Research (Hodgen and Wiliam 2006; Lee 2006; Clarke 2001) also suggests that for assessment activities to be successful they need to engage children in their own learning. For this to happen children need to understand the learning goal, their current position and how to close the gap between the two. Clarke (2001) argues that children can be supported in the process of 'closing the gap' through the use of 'success criteria'. Essentially success criteria list the steps that the children need to take in order to reach the learning outcome. Clarke recommends that success criteria are developed alongside children and that they can take a range of forms. This in turn means that the language used must be appropriate for the particular group of children for whom the learning objective is devised. To write success criteria for the learning intention 'find a small difference by counting up' in language appropriate for a particular year group criteria requires an understanding of the mathematical content.

It could also be argued (Aubrey 1997) that the diagnosis of misconceptions is another key feature of 'knowledge of learners' as, while it is important to find out what children do know and understand, it is equally important to find out where there may be gaps or weaknesses in children's understanding of mathematics. In order to define a misconception it is first necessary to consider the nature of conceptual development. Constructivist philosophy is underpinned by the notion that learning is the active construction of knowledge on the basis of what is already known. Misconceptions are sometimes (Drews 2005) described as alternative constructs of a situation based on limited experience of particular aspects of mathematics. For example, a child may construct the generalisation that 'you always subtract the smaller number from the larger number' based on their experience in subtracting natural numbers in a range of contexts. This would then be challenged when negative numbers are introduced or when a context demands that the larger number is subtracted from a smaller number. Askew and Wiliam (1994) argue that teachers should make specific efforts to provide learning opportunities which invite cognitive dissonance of this kind. This is reinforced by Swan (2001: 50) who suggests that misconceptions need to be made explicit, explored and discussed if long-term learning is to take place.

This section has illustrated that pedagogical content knowledge includes the ability to identify what pupils know and understand, and that teachers need a deep understanding of primary mathematics in order to build a full picture of pupil performance.

Reflective task

What do the children in your class understand about differing subtraction structures? How could you find out more?

Finally, it is clear that, as Aubrey (1997) argues, the quality of teachers' judgements are based on data gathered from individual responses to particular classroom tasks, there are a need for effective tasks which explore and expose the child's existing learning. A further conclusion that can be drawn is that assessment cannot be a 'bolt on' activity but should be an integral part of the teaching and learning process. This then leads to the next section in this chapter.

Effective task design

Before task design can be considered in further depth the choice of the term 'task' needs to be justified. Mason and Johnston-Wilder (2006: 5) note that the terms 'task' and 'activity' are often treated as synonyms but suggest that it is in fact important to draw a distinction between the two terms as 'the purpose of a *task* is to initiate *activity* by learners'. Further justification for the choice of terminology comes from the theories of learning which were identified in Chapter 3, that is, that children and adults construct their own understanding of mathematics. Mason and Johnston-Wilder (2006: 5) suggest that when undertaking a task 'learners construct and act upon objects, whether physical, mental or symbolic that pertain to a mathematical topic'. The purpose of setting the task is to actively engage children in the process of making sense of aspects of their world using their existing knowledge and understanding. Finally, in terms of justification, in Chapter 3 we identified 'big ideas' as one of the key features of subject knowledge. This has resonance with the proposition by Hiebert and Carpenter (2006: 5) that the task should 'draw learners' attention to important features, so that they may learn to distinguish between relevant aspects, or recognise properties, or appreciate relationships between properties'.

Hiebert *et al.* (1997: 31) also note that the teacher's role in setting tasks is more complex than simply devising individual tasks one after the other. Instead teachers need to devise sequences of tasks so that over time, students' experiences add up to 'something important'. Ofsted (2008) also suggest that one of the features of good mathematics teaching is that the lesson forms a part of a developmental sequence. Here then, again, we begin to see the 'intertwined' nature of subject knowledge and pedagogical content knowledge as, in order to meet this aim, teachers need to be able to trace mathematical progression (see previous chapter). A second point raised by Hiebert *et al.* (1997: 31) is that tasks should leave behind 'important residue'. Residue could be thought of (Davis 1992) as the learning that children take from solving problems which can be used in other situations. In the case of the example listed above, one 'important residue' could be an understanding of different subtraction structures. So once again subject knowledge and pedagogical content knowledge can be seen to be intertwined.

When designing a task the teacher has a number of important decisions to make in order to ensure that the task is effective. The next section will consider some of those decisions.

The first decision that teachers may wish to consider when designing a task is whether the task will be presented in context or not. Here again opinions are divided. Treffers and Beishuizen (1999) suggest that by adopting approaches advocated by Realistic Mathematics Education (RME) greater active pupil involvement in tasks can be achieved. RME is underpinned by the idea that by reversing the teaching and learning process so that children are required to find mathematical patterns and processes through the investigation of realistic mathematical situations, children become active participants in the learning process. Realistic contexts are used as starting points because they give pupils a better representation of the problem and a better mental image of their solution strategies at work, compared with bare number problems. For this reason context problems are preferably presented with a picture containing a modelling suggestion for the invited mathematical activity. The question posed in Figure 4.1 asks children to compare the height of Mount Everest and the height of Mount Snowdon and invites the calculation 8872 – 1085 using a counting-up structure.

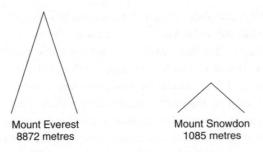

Mount Everest
8872 metres

Mount Snowdon
1085 metres

■ **Figure 4.1** Finding the difference. How much taller is Mount Everest?

This calculation may be perceived as too difficult for children who are not familiar with the procedures for subtraction of two four-digit numbers. However, van den Heuvel-Panhuizen (1999: 132) suggests that many children who cannot solve the bare problem could solve this context problem. The reason that she gives for this is that the context elicits a complementary addition strategy for the subtraction task. The question could also be posed in language which suggests 'take away' which would then encourage a child to adopt a counting back or partitioning method (e.g. *A bookshop had 346 copies of the new Harry Potter book. 27 were sold in one hour. How many were left?*). In other words the transmission of a method by the teacher is not necessary as the process can be anticipated by the child. According to RME, learning can best take place by offering pupils context problems in which they can discern mathematical procedures through 'guided reinvention' (Treffers and Beishuizen 1999: 31).

The counter-argument to this could be that the context is a distraction from the key mathematical content. In some cases it might even be the case that the context in which children encounter a particular concept may not always exactly follow the structure of the number system or that the language associated with the context can mask the relationships that exist between different numbers. For example, if money is used to explore the context of place value then children will read £1.80 as one pound and eighty pence. The children may develop an understanding of £1 as the whole but may not recognise 80p as 8/10 of the whole. Teaching through this context may also hinder progression as the potential to consider thousandths in this context is not possible. It could therefore be argued that in order to develop a complete under-standing of the various subtraction structures, or indeed to develop a fascination for numbers, children should work with numbers in their own right. In the context of subtraction children need to be able to make a decision about whether to complete a calculation by counting up or counting back. In order to do this the child needs to know whether the two numbers are 'close together' or 'far apart'. This would suggest that children need to develop a 'feel for numbers' or 'number sense'. This might include the ability to visualise the relative size (or position on a number line) of numbers or amounts which can only be achieved by considering numbers in their own right (rather than in context).

Another key feature of task design is the examples that are selected for pupils to consider. The examples that a teacher chooses have the potential to lead to either appropriate or invalid generalisations and to challenge or confirm pupil understanding. For example, a teacher who consistently chooses to show children examples of right angles where horizontal and vertical lines meet may inadvertently lead children to make the generalisation that this is the definition of a right angle. Conversely, a teacher who asks 'what about $6 \times \frac{1}{2}$' challenges pupil perception that 'multiplication makes the answer bigger'. One way to address invalid generalisations could be to design sorting tasks. Askew and Wiliam (1995) note that an important category in any kind of sorting activity should be 'nearly' examples. Pupils could be asked to sort a series of angles into those which are right angles, those which are not right angles and those which are 'nearly' right angles, and children sorting subtraction questions would need to consider those that are neither very close together or very far apart. Mason and Watson (2005) and Mason and Johnston-Wilder (2006) take this one step further with the idea that asking children to decide on their own examples can be of benefit to learners. So if when undertaking a task such as the ones listed above, children were asked to note where they ran into conflict they could then be asked to make a set of cards that they think might produce further discussion.

Reflective task

Critically evaluate the task listed below based on the key criteria for an effective task:

> The task should draw learners' attention to the important features of mathematics.

> The task should leave behind 'important residue'.

Sort these calculations in different ways:

$32 - 3$	$2001 - 1998$	$138 - 135$	$138 - 99$	$17 + 6$
$2001 - 5$	$138 - 42$	$29 + 3$	$32 - 13$	$32 - 29$

In your role of mathematics specialist teacher you may collaborate with other teachers in designing effective tasks or considering ways in which current practice in lesson planning could be developed to enrich classroom experiences for children.

Resources/representations/analogies/demonstrations and explanations/questions/discussion

This section will discuss the need for teachers to make use of a range of resources, representations and analogies alongside appropriate explanations and questions in order to transform personal deep subject knowledge into a form that is accessible to learners.

Orton and Frobisher (1996) argue that teaching by exposition alone is ineffective. This leads them to the conclusion that resources/representations/analogies/demonstrations are needed alongside explanations, questions and discussion. The converse is also true; models and images alone are ineffective. It is the explanations/questions and discussion that are used alongside them that are key to promoting understanding. In her exploration of Chinese and US teachers' approaches to teaching subtraction Ma (1999: 5) found that many teachers stated that providing a hands-on experience, using a range of resources, would facilitate better learning than just telling. However, she goes on to warn that 'a good vehicle, however does not guarantee the right destination', i.e. the way in which resources are used depends on the mathematical understanding of the teacher using them. Hence the two ideas of choice of models and images and teacher exploration and explanation are considered together in this section.

Rowland *et al.* (2009) also note that physical and pictorial representations are widely used in order to support the teaching and learning of mathematics. One reason for this could be that, as Bruner (1974) suggests, images act as an intermediary between the concrete and the abstract. For example, while it is not possible to represent negative numbers in any concrete form we can use images and analogies to represent negative numbers. Bruner suggested three modes of representation: enactive, iconic and symbolic. An enactive representation requires physical action; iconic representations make use of pictorial images and diagrams; and symbolic representations allow mental manipulation.

The 'take away' structure of subtraction would seem to be the most straightforward to illustrate. It could be represented in an enactive way, i.e. by using physical objects to represent the initial quantity, then removing the required quantity and counting what is left. It could also be represented on a number line which could be either an iconic representation (i.e. a 'picture' of part of the number system) or if children are required to either move objects or jump along a number line it could be described as an enactive representation. The associated mathematical notation can be modelled alongside the action of 'taking away' the objects or counting back on the number line.

Difference is more complex.

Reflective task

Consider the following resources/scenarios alongside the question 32 – 29.

How does each image or scenario support (or not) an understanding of:

a the 'idea' of subtraction as 'difference'?

b the associated mathematical vocabulary?

c the associated mathematical notation?

Images and scenarios

1 Start with 29 multi-link. Add on multi-link until 32 is reached. Count the multi-link that need to be added.

2 Build two multi-link towers of different heights and possibly different colours. Count the difference.

3 Devise a number line with 32 labelled divisions. Cut off, strike through or 'take away' 29. Count what is left.

4 Use a number line to calculate 32 – 29 by counting back or 'taking away'. Next calculate 32 – 29 by counting up. Note that in both cases the answer is 3.

5 Pose the question as: 'What is the difference between 32 and 29?'

6 Pose the question as: 'John has 29 marbles and Peter has 32. How many more marbles does Peter have?'

Whether subtraction is considered as 'take away' or 'difference' the answer will be the same but the representation, even when using the same resource, will be different. It has already been noted that the use of resources or representations is far from independent from explanations and questions used by the teacher; indeed Rowland *et al.* (2009: 22) suggest that being able to explain aspects of mathematics in ways that children will understand is an essential part of successful teaching.

Questioning is a two-way process. There is a plethora of research evidence which identifies the importance of effective teacher questioning and outlines the range of different questioning techniques that a teacher might consider. For example, a teacher might use diagnostic questions which are written to explore children's thinking, or a teacher might ask a question that initiates debate by introducing conflicting ideas, or a teacher might ask closed questions in order to reinforce 'known facts'. However, Ma (1999) also suggests that when using images and resources children may raise questions themselves which have the potential to lead to a deeper understanding of mathematics. She also draws attention to the fact that the realisation of the learning potential of these questions relies on the quality of the teacher's understanding of the subject matter. For example, when exploring rotational and line symmetry of 2-D shapes a child may ask: 'Is it true that shapes always have the same number of lines of symmetry as order of rotational symmetry?' This provides a useful avenue for enquiry but a teacher would need confidence in his/her subject knowledge in order to pursue the child's line of thought.

Ofsted (2008) consider a third strand of effective questioning and discussion: the quality of pupil responses to questions posed. They suggest that good primary mathematics teachers expect children to give explanations of their reasoning (rather than simply the method used) and that teachers should challenge pupils if their explanations do not reflect their ability.

So far these three aspects of pedagogical knowledge have been considered in isolation. However, there are a number of links between these ideas. For example it would seem reasonable to suggest that knowledge of learners could not be gained without a rich discussion of a mathematical task or that effective tasks cannot be introduced to children without appropriate discussion or explanation.

The three questions below are designed to provide an opportunity for you to consider further the links between the three strands of pedagogical knowledge.

Reflective task

Making links between aspects of pedagogical knowledge

> a Knowledge of learners *and* resources/representations/analogies/demonstrations and explanations/questions/discussion

What resources would you use to explore, expose and address the invalid generalisation that the larger the object is the heavier it is?

> b Knowledge of learners *and* effective task design

Design a task which integrates opportunities for assessing pupil understanding with rich mathematical discussion.

> c Effective task design *and* resources/representations/analogies/demonstrations and explanations/questions/discussion

Design a task which uses an image (real or imagined) as a starting point for discussion.

SUBJECT KNOWLEDGE AND PEDAGOGICAL KNOWLEDGE

In Chapters 3 and 4 of this book we separated subject knowledge and pedagogical content knowledge in order to provide an opportunity for teachers to consider these two key ideas in detail. The final section of this chapter will return to the idea presented at the beginning of Chapter 4, that a teacher's knowledge is pedagogically situated: situated in and stemming from the classroom.

Reflective task

Reflect on your response to the question posed at the start of this chapter. Is there a clear distinction between Shulman's categories of subject matter content knowledge and pedagogical content knowledge? Has your thinking changed?

The following sections consider some links between deep subject knowledge of each of the three key themes that comprise pedagogical knowledge.

Links between deep subject knowledge and 'knowledge of learners'

We suggested in Chapter 2 that teachers with deep subject knowledge would be able to identify key mathematical ideas (rather than those that lie on the periphery). It would seem sensible to suggest that teachers would want to know about pupil understanding of big ideas (rather that those which lie on the periphery).

It could be argued that the assessment of children's relational understanding (Skemp 1989) of mathematics and their ability to reason between ideas (Barmby *et al.* 2009) should also be key features of a teacher's 'knowledge of learners'. The link between the 'making connections' strand of deep subject knowledge and knowledge of learners is evident here. A further potential link could be that the notion of connectedness also includes the connected nature of planning, teaching and assessment.

We also included the diagnosis of errors and misconceptions under the heading 'knowledge of learners'. This has clear links with the 'tracing mathematical progression' as identification of prior learning in order to make an accurate diagnosis is clearly necessary, as is an understanding of next steps in order to plan appropriate remediation tasks. Indeed, these links are clearly raised in the content of the previous chapter.

Links between deep subject knowledge and effective task design

The previous chapter identified 'tracing mathematical progression' as a key feature of deep subject knowledge. This chapter noted that effective task design included an ability to devise sequences of tasks. The link between subject knowledge and pedagogical content knowledge is clear, as one cannot be achieved without the other. It is also important to consider links with using and applying mathematics and with making mathematical connections. In designing effective tasks teachers with deep subject knowledge will recognise the need for the task to provide opportunities for children to both develop an understanding of a range of mathematical processes and make connections between ideas.

Links between deep subject knowledge and resources/representations/ analogies/demonstrations and explanations/questions/discussion

The intertwined nature of subject and pedagogical knowledge is again clear. The representations, analogies or explanations that a teacher chooses depend on the purpose of the lesson. If the purpose includes the intention for children to make connections between different aspects of mathematics or to use and apply mathematics then this will influence choice of representation or analogies.

Reflective task

Consider the images a teacher might choose to use in order to make the links between different operations clear? For example, consider the images you use to illustrate the nature of addition and those which you use to illustrate multiplication. Do the models and images also provide an opportunity to consider the links between the two operations?

There are also links with 'tracing mathematical progression' and 'identifying key ideas' with representations. A teacher with a deep understanding of mathematical progression would choose to use models and images that do not lead children down blind alleys or mathematical dead ends, but instead allow children to develop a complete understanding of a concept. The work of Barmby *et al.* (2009) on the use of the array is a good example of this. They argue that any representation of an aspect of mathematics should meet two key criteria: the representation must illustrate the full range of characteristics of the concept and aid calculation. They go on to compare representations of multiplication which focus on repeated addition with representations of multiplication as an array. They analyse the success of each representation in modelling key features of multiplication. While images of repeated addition (such as the number line) do demonstrate the binary nature of multiplication they do not clearly represent commutativity or distributivity. As commutativity or distributivity are the principles on which approaches to both mental and written methods of calculation depend it is evident that the choice of models of multiplication which illustrate repeated addition does not provide children with a complete picture of the features of the concept or support children in making progress with this operation. A similar argument could be made with the choice of multi-link as a resource to model the operation of addition. While this model is useful to illustrate aggregation (the joining of two sets) it may be less useful in exploring augmentation (counting on).

CONCLUSIONS

This chapter has been written to challenge you to analyse your understanding of pedagogy and to make connections between subject knowledge and pedagogical knowledge. These key questions reflect the ideas that have been raised.

In the area of mathematics which you will teach next in your classroom:

■ What do the learners of mathematics in your class know about the key ideas which compose the chosen aspect of mathematics?
■ What tasks will you prepare for children that initiate activity by the learner and allow them to make progress along learning trajectories?
■ What analogies/representations/explanations or resources will you use to illustrate key ideas?

In this chapter we have identified features of pedagogical knowledge in the context of mathematics. We have discussed knowledge of learners, effective mathematical tasks and images and analogies for learning. Chapters 6, 7 and 8 will consider each of these features in the areas of multiplication, time and data handling, allowing you to reflect on what each might mean in your school in the context of a specific area of mathematics.

FURTHER READING

Mason, J. and Johnston-Wilder, S. (2006) *Designing and Using Mathematical Tasks.* Hatfield: Tarquin. This book considers mathematical tasks and the nature of mathematical activity in some depth. It also makes use of a range of examples to illustrate these points.

Aubrey, C. (1997) *Mathematics Teaching in the Early Years: An Investigation of Teachers' Subject Knowledge.* London: Falmer Press. This book considers the links between subject knowledge and practice. While it is focused on the early years in particular, the key ideas can be extended across the primary phase.

Hodgen, J. and Wiliam, D. (2006) *Mathematics Inside the Black Box: Assessment for Learning in the Mathematics Classroom.* London: NFER Nelson. This document takes a mathematics-specific look at issues to do with assessment for learning.

CHAPTER 5

LEADING PROFESSIONAL LEARNING IN MATHEMATICS IN YOUR SCHOOL; MENTORING AND COACHING

The Williams Review (2008: 7) recommended that, 'There should be at least one Mathematics Specialist in each primary school'. The specialist teacher is expected to fulfil a specific personal and job specification that includes 'Act as peer-to-peer coach and mentor and support the mathematical professional development of serving teachers, NQTs, ITT students on placement and teaching assistants within the school' (p. 20). The purpose of this chapter is to help you to consider developing the learning and teaching of mathematics not just in your own class or the classes you directly teach but across the entire school. Nearly all primary teachers are generalist, some have special interest in a particular curriculum area but you are likely to be the only mathematics specialist in your school. This is a great responsibility and will take time and sensitivity to develop. Communicating enthusiasm for the subject will also be vitally important. Williams suggested that much of the work of supporting other teachers and staff members would be done through mentoring and coaching.

This chapter aims to:

- help you to reflect on your role as a mathematics specialist teacher (MaST) in supporting the learning and teaching of mathematics across your school;
- help you to consider what mentoring and coaching are and where your role as a MaST fits with these ideas;
- help you to think about different approaches and models you might use;
- consider the principles of mentoring and coaching;
- help you to think about and develop the skills and activities needed for mentoring and coaching;

■   identify the support you will need in the role and the benefits you might gain from it for your own professional development.

Reflective task

Think about your own professional development from when you very first started learning to teach until now. What types of activities have been particularly effective for you? Why do you think those activities have been more successful than some others? How might this impact on the way you want to work with other teachers and staff in your school to improve the learning and teaching of mathematics?

WHAT IS MENTORING AND WHAT IS COACHING?

Reflective task

What do the terms mentoring and coaching mean to you? How are they similar and how are they different?

The term mentoring has been in use in schools for some time now, especially in relation to supporting student teachers on placements; coaching is newer in this context. Increasingly, the two words are being used together to make one term 'mentoringandcoaching', a little like 'giftedandtalented'.

Literature provides many different definitions of mentoring and coaching and to some extent they are overlapping and contradictory. However, some similarities can be identified within the separate definitions. Both ideas relate to learning contexts mainly over a period of time and with a one-to-one relationship between mentor or coach and mentee or coachee. The terms mentee and coachee are clumsy and difficult, so for this chapter we have chosen to use the term professional learner to refer to the member of staff who is receiving the mentoring or coaching.

Many of the definitions of mentoring refer to a more experienced colleague working with a less experienced one, particularly at a specific transition point in a career, such as initial teacher education, the Newly Qualified Teacher period, becoming a headteacher, thus implying that the mentor has successfully achieved this transition before and has specific knowledge and expertise to offer the less experienced teacher (Garvey 2010; Bubb and Earley 2010; Wright 2010; Kerry and Shelton Mayes 1995; Shaw 1995; Pollard 2008; Allison and Harbour 2009). Often definitions of mentoring include some reference to instructing or giving advice (Garvey 2010; Bubb and Earley 2010; Wright 2010; Allison and Harbour 2009).

In contrast to this, coaching is often seen as non-hierarchical and about facilitating, questioning and drawing out answers rather than giving them (Bubb and Earley 2010; Allison and Harbour 2009; Garvey 2010). However, Brockbank and McGill (2006) refer to dictionary definitions of 'coach' which include the terms 'instructor', 'teacher', 'trainer', 'giving instructions' as well as 'professional adviser'.

Allison and Harbour (2009) see the relationship between mentoring and coaching as a continuum of support and development. Garvey (2010) implies that the differences between the terms are not important and that possibly another term will be found to include both ideas; in the meantime he suggests that description of the activity may be more helpful than definition and refers to 'purposeful conversations'. Going further than this, Pask and Joy (2007) suggest that trying to distinguish between mentoring and coaching is actually unhelpful; their book entitled *Mentoring-Coaching: A Guide for Education Professionals* emphasises the importance of what they call 'the crucial hyphen'.

CUREE provides two definitions of coaching, one referred to as specialist coaching, defined as 'A structured, sustained process between two or more professional learners to enable them to embed new knowledge and skills from specialist sources in day-to-day practice' (DfES 2005). The subject expertise developed within the MaST course would indicate that the specialist coach would impart some knowledge and skills to the teacher they are working with and therefore moves the activity along Allison and Harbour's (2010) continuum towards mentoring from coaching. The subject-specific, targeted nature of the activity and the fact that the MaST would not necessarily be senior to the teacher(s) they are working with would both imply that the activity is coaching.

Therefore the CUREE definition of specialist coach is helpful in defining the role of the MaST and in many ways it sits between mentoring and coaching as defined by Garvey (2010) and Wright (2010). As long as 'purposeful conversations' are taking place to improve the learning and teaching of mathematics in your school, perhaps the distinction between mentoring and coaching does not matter. However, in analysing the activity more closely and in order to maximise effectiveness, it is useful to break this down to identify areas of strength and areas for improvement and development. Ofsted (2010b) support this in their report *Good Professional Development in Schools*, saying 'The survey schools used the terms "coaching" and "mentoring" extensively but there was no common understanding of what they meant.' The report goes on to say, 'because they did not have a clear understanding of the different forms coaching and mentoring could take, they did not always use them to best effect'. Their definitions also sub-divide coaching into 'expert coaching', when the coach has expertise in the skill being developed and 'peer coaching', when colleagues work collaboratively to develop something of benefit to them both.

APPROACHES TO COACHING

Brockbank and McGill (2006) identify three approaches to coaching that can be used within different contexts and for different purposes. These are labelled Functionalist, Engagement and Evolutionary.

Reflective task

Read through these short summary definitions of Brockbank and McGill's approaches to coaching. Which of these have you used in the past? Which would you like to aim to use in your role as a mathematics specialist teacher?

Functionalist coaching – learning for improvement that is based on factual learning and aims to maintain the status quo within an organisation; this involves mainly telling.

Engagement coaching – 'seeks to persuade the client to adopt the learning objectives of the organisation or system' (p. 96); this may be used where improving performance in an unpopular activity is required; therefore a more humanistic approach is needed than with functionalist coaching.

Evolutionary coaching – the professional learner defines their own goals and takes ownership of their learning, leading to transformation.

MODELS OF COACHING

Different models of coaching have also been proposed. These can be helpful in structuring and analysing a coaching episode. One of the simplest to remember is the GROW model, which was developed by Whitmore in 1996 and outlined by Brockbank and McGill (2006). It starts from the idea that coaching is about unlocking people's potential and helping them to learn rather than teaching them. The letters represent the different stages of the process:

■ G – establish the goal
■ R – examine the reality
■ O – consider all options
■ W – confirm the will to act

(Brockbank and McGill 2006: 138)

Another model, again outlined by Brockbank and McGill, that mathematics specialist teachers might find helpful is the Flow model, which was developed by Flaherty in 1999:

1 Establish relationship
2 Recognise opening
3 Observe/assess
4 Enrol client
5 Coaching conversations

(Brockbank and McGill 2006: 142)

Reflective task

Do you think either of these models would be useful in your coaching in school? Which one will you choose to use? Will it depend on the context?

PRINCIPLES OF MENTORING AND COACHING

CUREE (DfES 2005), as described above, put forward a definition of mentoring and two for coaching, one of which was the role of the specialist coach, which fits most neatly with the role of the mathematics specialist teacher. They also proposed some principles of effective mentoring and coaching; interestingly these principles apply to mentoring and to coaching activity.

Reflective task

Think about the important principles of mentoring and coaching activity from your own point of view. List some principles and then compare your list to those put forward by CUREE and the 2005 National Framework for Mentoring and Coaching.

Ten principles

Effective coaching and mentoring involves:

- a learning conversation
- a learning agreement
- growing self-direction
- understanding why different approaches work
- experimenting and observing
- a thoughtful relationship
- combining support from fellow professional learners and specialists
- setting challenging and personal goals
- acknowledging the benefits to the mentors and coaches
- using resources effectively.

(DfES 2005)

Burley and Pomphrey (2011: 36) have argued that these are not principles but rather a 'useful list for describing mentoring and coaching relationships and activity'.

This may mean that this list is quite different from your own created in the reflective task.

SKILLS OF COACHING

Due to the overlapping nature of the ideas of mentoring and coaching it is possible that requisite skills may overlap and be used effectively in both situations; they may however be used to a greater or lesser extent.

Learning conversations will form a key part in professional development through coaching. It is through these that ideas are articulated, discussed, reviewed and refined. They are important in setting the tone and the direction at the beginning, as they help to establish the trust and respect that the coaching relationship is based on. They are also important at the end of the coaching episode to sum up and reinforce the learning. Throughout they can be used to support the professional learner in assuming greater responsibility for their own learning and development.

Two of the practical considerations about learning conversations concern when and where the conversation will take place. Confidentiality is very important. In some schools it is difficult to find a space to have a private conversation, so this may need thought and planning. When the conversation takes place is also important. If it is a debrief conversation after a lesson observation, it is helpful if it does not take place immediately after the lesson as this gives time for reflection before the conversation; however, it may lose some of its value if there is too long between the observation and the conversation as both observer and observed may begin to forget aspects of the lesson that would benefit from discussion.

The purpose of the coaching should be established and clear for yourself and the professional learner from the beginning; this is not a performance management situation. The purpose is specifically to improve the learning and teaching of an aspect of mathematics within the school. Ground rules should be set, as this helps to increase trust between yourself and the professional learner; they must be sure that you are not going to report aspects of conversations in the staff room or the head teacher's office. Establishing this trust means that the professional learner is more likely to be open to improvement by being more honest about the starting point. One of the ways of encouraging this is through demonstrating empathy in order to truly understand the professional learner's point of view and to plan effectively for progress.

Just as when you teach the children in your class, you need to assess and clarify the professional learner's needs to decide on what is appropriate next. The best way to do this is through listening actively and carefully as they describe where they are. You will need to ask the right open questions in order to understand the situation fully and to establish what the teacher wishes to gain from the coaching episode. This also helps the professional learner to take and feel ownership of the process, thus contributing to commitment to change and improvement. Summing up orally at the end of the conversation will also help to ensure that you have a joint understanding of the situation and the way forward.

Sensitive questioning in a learning conversation can promote reflection. The opposite is also true; asking an inappropriate question can close down thinking and lead to greater reliance.

Professional learners may value support in setting appropriate and specific goals and identifying and assessing different options for obtaining those; once again the professional learner's ownership is important here and this is very much linked to the paragraph above about listening.

Linked to the point above, sometimes as a mentor or coach it can be tempting to think that once you have agreed a goal or a target, the teacher can and will just get on with achieving it. However, it is not always that simple; often a series of steps may be required in order to achieve a specific goal and you may need to support identification of the steps and development of an action plan.

Throughout the coaching process you will be engaged in reflection and joint reflection with the professional learner. In teaching we often consider that reflection is an important aspect of an effective teacher's practice.

Reflective task

Consider these questions before reading a quotation from Pollard about reflection and reflective teaching. What is reflection? Do you think it is important for a teacher? Why?

Teaching is a complex and highly skilled activity which, above all, requires classroom teachers to exercise judgement in deciding how to act. High quality teaching, and thus pupil learning, is dependent on the existence of such professional expertise … The process of reflective teaching supports the development and maintenance of professional expertise … The process of reflection thus feeds a constructive spiral of professional development and capability.

(Pollard 2008: 5)

COACHING ACTIVITIES

As a mathematics specialist teacher and specialist coach you will be involved in a number of activities; all of these will be supported by or will centre on coaching conversations and therefore involve many or all of the skills detailed in the previous section.

In order to model expertise in a specific aspect of mathematics, you may run demonstration lessons. This may come from a request from another teacher or it may be something you suggest in a conversation with a teacher. One of the advantages of this is that the watching teacher need not feel under pressure as you are the one being observed, not them, although a small minority of teachers feel that observing others is not good use of their time. Some may also feel patronised by being asked or told to observe someone else. Sensitive handling of the conversation is therefore necessary. Preparation for a demonstration lesson is very important. You will want the lesson to be effective for the learning of the observing teacher and for the children involved. It is useful if the professional learner has a copy of a lesson plan or notes to refer to during the lesson, but don't worry if you deviate from it, you can discuss this later. It may also be useful if in advance of the lesson you have discussed what the professional learner wants to get out of the lesson and the way they might record their observations. (You may also like a copy of their notes.) Remember to check that all resources are well prepared for the lesson and that any support staff are also briefed. Children may also want to know why there is a visitor in their classroom.

Reflective task

Prepare a check list for yourself of things to consider when teaching a demonstration lesson. Would you need to consider additional factors if you teach a class other than your own?

At other times you may be involved in watching others teach. In this situation trust and confidentiality are paramount. In advance of the lesson, both you and the observed teacher need to be very clear about the purpose of the observation and what will happen with the information gathered in the observation. Obviously as a mathematics specialist teacher, your job is to improve the quality of learning and teaching within mathematics within your school and this must always be at the forefront of your mind when observing. As you are aiming to do this in a supportive way, it would be highly unusual to observe mathematics lessons without prior arrangement. It is also important at the planning stage to decide when, where and how a follow-up conversation will take place as this is a key learning opportunity. Decisions will also need to be taken as to what your role will be in the classroom during the lesson. Will you just sit and watch? Will you work with a group of children in part of the lesson? Will you circulate round the class and talk to children as they are engaged in their mathematics? Will your role change during the lesson? How will you record what you see? If you have decided that the debrief conversation will happen at a later time, do remember to say a quick positive comment to the teacher before leaving the lesson; this may reassure them and continue to foster the positive relationship that is so important.

Reflective task

How will you begin the post-lesson conversation? What principles will you adhere to?

Many mentors like to start a learning conversation by asking the professional learner how they think the lesson went. However, there is a danger in this approach of the learner listing all the aspects they were not pleased with or perceived that they went wrong; this can lead to a negative conversation. Asking learners to focus on something they were pleased with first can help to create a positive tone to the conversation.

Shared learning experiences through observation, possibly supported by video, can be useful starting points for discussion. Video can be paused to enable discussion to take place at interesting points; it can also be useful for you and the professional learner to watch the video separately before the conversation session, to prepare which points you would both want to discuss in the session.

Many teachers find collaboration a useful form of professional learning – did you have this on your list at the beginning of the chapter? Collaboration can take place in a number of forms; it might include all or any of: joint planning, teaching and evaluation of a lesson or lessons. The collaboration may be equal between the two collaborators or unequal.

Collaborative planning can lead to well-thought-out lessons which engage the children effectively and lead to learning and progress. Teachers often find it helpful to discuss ideas for lessons and can often bounce ideas around and learn from each other.

Collaborative teaching can be enjoyable and lead again to better lessons; the children often find it more interesting and enjoyable too. They can also benefit from more attention, individual and small-group or specialist whole-class teaching. Teachers will often be motivated to work even harder during a collaborative lesson than they would on their own.

Collaborative evaluation will follow naturally from observing each other, collaborative planning and teaching. It would be almost impossible not to discuss the lesson afterwards! However, your job will be to focus the discussion and make sure that the maximum benefit is derived from the experience in terms of the future learning and teaching of mathematics.

You may also be involved in supporting planning in a more distant way that may not be considered as collaborative. This could involve providing a long-term or outline plan for teachers to plan from in the medium to short term. It may also be that teachers give you some mathematics planning that you are asked to comment on and provide feedback on. This is a good opportunity to check that progression is planned for and to give advice and suggestions on suitable resources and approaches. It may also mean attending a team meeting where teachers are involved in planning mathematics lessons so you are able to be consulted and again given the opportunity to make suggestions and give advice.

As a result of some of the activities detailed above and from various other conversations that you have with members of staff about mathematics learning and teaching you will support aspects of subject knowledge. Rowland *et al.* (2009) identified the knowledge quartet that they argue all teachers need in order to teach mathematics effectively. This can be helpful knowledge for you as you try to analyse your own and other teachers' subject knowledge and to boost it appropriately and effectively. The members of the quartet are:

■ foundation, which includes mathematical knowledge and beliefs about mathematics;
■ transformation, which is about teachers' choices of ways of making the mathematics accessible to children;
■ connection, which includes ideas of progression and making connections between different mathematical ideas;
■ contingency, which involves responding appropriately to children and unexpected opportunities.

They are linked to Shulman's (1986) earlier work on the seven categories of teacher knowledge, but are developed from observations of mathematics lessons. Part of your response to observing and analysing others' practice may be providing information, for example about appropriate resources that might support the transformation and making mathematics accessible to the children. Your response may also be to facilitate access to research about the learning and teaching of mathematics that will help a professional learner to support the learning and teaching in their own class more effectively. More details of this work can be found in Chapter 3.

Lesson study was suggested in the Williams Review (2008) as a cost-effective way for mathematics specialist teachers to support professional learning and improvements in the learning and teaching of the subject in their schools. The idea originated from Japan, but has spread round the world in different forms. In Japan, lesson study often takes place in large groups. The National Strategies (DCSF 2007) have adopted the ideas here but recommend groups of three teachers undertaking the lesson study. The first step in lesson study is to identify a group of teachers who are likely to be enthusiastic about the approach. These teachers work together collaboratively to determine a focus for the lesson study. They plan the study lesson together with a particular group of pupils in mind. One of the teachers teaches the lesson, the others observe, focusing on the learning of particular focus pupils. The lesson is jointly evaluated later, often including interviewing focus pupils to gain their perspective on the learning. In order to sustain and develop improvement through this approach it is helpful then to plan and teach another lesson study and to share the outcomes with colleagues. Although this has been identified as a cost-effective approach to continuing professional development, there are implications for use of time in school in order to release teachers to be available at the same time for planning, teaching and evaluation.

During many of the activities listed above, certainly the more formal, planned and longer-term coaching episodes, there will be notes of the activities. There may be a school policy about what should happen to notes, who has ownership of them and what purposes they will be used for. However, it is important that a professional learner is clear and comfortable about the destination of any notes and has a copy of them.

OVERCOMING BARRIERS AND SUPPORT FOR COACHING

Coaching is most effective when the professional learner wants to be coached and there is support for the coaching from the senior management team and head teacher in the school. Many mathematics specialist teachers have the full support of their head teacher and the head teacher will actively wish to support the teacher in their work to improve the mathematics learning and teaching within the school. These head teachers, having invested in this support, would also wish to provide some non-contact time for the mathematics specialist teacher to be able to work with other teachers and staff in the school. Although some support can and should be provided informally and unofficially outside of lesson time, in order to maximise the benefits of having a mathematics specialist teacher, time needs to be provided. If you are feeling frustrated and unsupported, try to meet with your head teacher or other senior management team member to talk through the issues and sort something out. Sensitively pointing out the benefits and linking to the school improvement plan can be a useful approach. Naturally, the head teacher and senior management team are likely to require feedback on the impact of the work later.

Teachers and other members of staff may approach you for support with mathematics teaching. This relies on the teachers knowing about your enthusiasm, interest and expertise in the area and perceiving you as open to approaches and respecting you as trustworthy and willing to help and support in a positive and constructive way. Once they have approached you and feel that the outcome was worthwhile, they will be encouraged to approach again.

Although it was not conceived in this way in the Williams Review (2008), sometimes a mathematics specialist teacher may be asked to 'sort out' a particular issue in mathematics teaching and learning in a specific class. This can be a challenging situation. Literature on mentoring and coaching refers to positive relationships being established between coach and professional learner and the professional learner having ownership of the process. Sensitive handling of the situation is clearly required here. The purposes of the process should be clear and coaching should not be confused with performance management.

OTHER PROFESSIONAL DEVELOPMENT ACTIVITIES

As a mathematics specialist teacher you may be involved in leading professional development in your school that does not come under the heading of mentoring or coaching. This may include leading staff meetings with groups of teachers, teaching assistants or a whole staff. Indeed, this can be a good way of tackling an awkward issue such as one particular teacher who is resistant to coaching because they feel threatened; in a staff meeting it is possible to introduce activities and facilitate discussions to depersonalise a situation and to include other more positive people in trying to get the message across. These meetings can also be a starting point, where staff members are challenged to 'have-a-go' at a particular type of activity and bring something back to a future meeting to discuss, evaluate and refine. They could also be a starting point for setting up study pairs or groups to look at and try aspects of mathematics pedagogy in more detail and to offer opportunities for coaching.

COACHING AND YOUR OWN PROFESSIONAL DEVELOPMENT

Reflective task

Think about the experiences of mentoring or coaching you have had. Have they been beneficial to your own professional development as well as for the person you have worked with? What made them beneficial for you as well?

Informally and anecdotally, many teachers involved in mentoring and coaching report that it is positive for their own professional development. This is also supported by my own experience of observing others teaching, children learning and of talking to others about learning and teaching. When we are involved in these activities we reflect on our own practice, we question ourselves and this often leads to us rethinking and trying something new or in a slightly different way. Coaching is a useful management skill and many coaches can use this skill to develop themselves as managers and aim for promotion in their career if they wish.

CASE STUDIES

Emma, a mathematics specialist teacher, was leading the updating of the school's long-term planning for mathematics as it had been decided to move away from the Primary National Strategy (DfES 2006) blocks and units that had previously been used. She was keen to make sure that lines of progression and links were clear in the document and that children were enabled to develop relational understanding (Skemp 1989). She decided to start with counting and place value, and arranged a staff meeting to begin the process as she was very keen that all teachers should be involved and feel ownership of the plans. She invited a tutor from the local university to come and run a training session in this area. This included consideration of how children learn to count and then how they progress with counting in steps of different sizes. The ideas of place value were then considered, including Thompson and Bramald's (2002) research into children's understanding of place value alongside the understanding they need in order to calculate mentally and later with formal written calculations.

In the following staff meeting, teachers were asked to bring resources from their classrooms that they used in teaching counting and place value for sorting and possible redistribution or ordering of new resources as appropriate. During the meeting they were also required to write on small, separate sheets of paper what they do with their class in their particular age group for counting and place value. These sheets were laid out in order along the floor in the staff room. The lines of progression were then critically considered, gaps identified, anomalies discussed and ironed out. Resources were matched to stages of the progression.

Thompson and Bramald's research was new to some members of staff, particularly Rachel, a Year 2 teacher. She had previously done lots of work with her Year 2 children, trying to get them to understand place value as column value. Rachel talked to Emma about this as she felt her children might benefit from working on quantity value at this age and together they decided to change this approach and try to do more work on quantity value with the Year 2s. They set up a separate meeting to plan the way forward.

Emma and Rachel read through Thompson and Bramald's research report prior to their meeting and then discussed it together. They decided first to audit the resources available in Rachel's class to make sure they were appropriate in supporting the development of understanding of quantity value. They decided that place value or arrow cards were going to be important and needed sorting out to ensure complete sets were easily accessible for all of the children. They then planned together a series of lessons on this area. Emma negotiated with the head teacher some release time from her own class so that they could team-teach one of the lessons. After some initial practical work involving counting out large numbers of objects and bundling into tens, children were asked to partition numbers such as $58 = 50 + 8$. The children seemed to pick the ideas up quite quickly and some were able to move on to partitioning three-digit numbers. Some children struggled with partitioning the numbers between 10 and 20. After the team-taught lesson, Emma and Rachel evaluated it together. They adjusted the planning for the next few lessons for Rachel's class, including more work on 11–20, then moving on to using these ideas with addition and subtraction. They also reviewed the long-term plans for the school to ensure that at a later date the children would meet the ideas of column value to support them when undertaking formal written calculations.

Reflecting later on the process, Emma was happy with how the coaching episode had gone. Rachel and Emma already had a good relationship and Emma was happy that Rachel had approached her in this situation. She also felt that they had been able to develop the learning and teaching of place value in Rachel's class together and that the relationship had been peer to peer, but with some specialist input from herself. Considering the model of coaching she had used, she felt that the G and R stages of the GROW model had been quickly achieved by Rachel herself in response to the training session arranged by Emma. In their first meeting after the two staff meetings they considered the options and it was easy to confirm the will to act in this case as Rachel was so open to moving forward in this way. In terms of the Flow model, the relationship was already in place, the opening was easy to recognise and very clear as Rachel approached Emma. Observing and assessment was also easy as Rachel had done this for herself; it was just a matter of Emma being clear for herself. The next stage of the Flow model, enrolling the client, similar to confirming the will to act in the GROW model, was also easy. Coaching conversations then took place before and after the team-taught lesson. Emma noted that the support and commitment of the head teacher and senior management team was important in enabling staff meeting time to be used for the development of mathematics and in allowing Emma release time from her own class in order to team-teach with Rachel.

Reflective task

To what extent do you agree with Emma's evaluation and reflection on her coaching episode?

Tony, a mathematics specialist teacher and mathematics co-ordinator, had been undertaking lesson observations across the school as part of the on-going monitoring of work. He noticed that the children in the reception class at his school seemed to be good at reciting number names in order, but he was concerned that they were less competent at counting out numbers of objects. The reception class teacher, Modupe, was new to the school and year group, having previously taught in Year 2 in another school for three years. Tony's own class was in Key Stage 2.

Modupe's lesson had started with the whole class on the carpet; they had been counting together in 1s, with Modupe pointing to the numerals on a number track as they counted. Then they recited the number rhyme 1, 2, Buckle my Shoe. The children then went off around the classroom and were engaged in a number of different activities, one of which was ordering numeral cards.

Tony and Modupe did not know each other very well, so Tony reflected on the best way of approaching Modupe about his concern as he wanted to establish a good working relationship and a successful outcome to the issue. He decided to emphasise the positive things he had noticed in Modupe's lesson, such as how good the children were at reciting number names in the correct order and how some of the children were beginning to recognise the numerals. He also talked to Modupe about his own lack of experience with 4–5-year-old children. He asked Modupe to outline her plans for the next few mathematics sessions for the class and she talked about getting the children to count up higher and to start counting backwards. He asked her about how good they were at counting out a number of objects, but Modupe seemed to think that counting was reciting number names in order and appeared surprised that there could be more to it. Tony asked if they could do some work together with her class in this area, emphasising that it would be good for him to learn more about how these young children learn. Modupe agreed and they arranged a meeting for the following week to plan a way forward.

Tony remembered that he had read about the work of Gelman and Gallistel, and the five counting principles that they put forward, in the book by Haylock and Cockburn (2008) that was kept on the bookshelves in the staff room. He decided to look this up in more detail so he could share the ideas with Modupe. He also referred to the Early Years Foundation Stage planning guidance to see what was expected in the curriculum for this age group. He gained agreement in principle from his head teacher to allow him some release time from his own class in order to team-teach alongside Modupe on one occasion.

During the meeting, Tony and Modupe discussed Gelman and Gallistel's five counting principles and the requirements for the curriculum. They decided to assess all of the children in the class against the first three principles: one-to-one correspondence, stable order and cardinal. Together they planned a series of playful activities where the children were asked to count a certain number of objects out of a large collection. Notes were kept for each child. Once all the assessments were complete, Tony and Modupe met again to discuss and evaluate the outcomes and to plan a way forward to help the children to progress. Interestingly, many of the children were confident with the stable order principle, at least up to 10 and many to 20 or beyond; however, they were not so good at one-to-one correspondence and certainly not as good with the cardinal principle.

Tony and Modupe planned activities for the children that would support them in this area. Many of the activities were playful and were for small groups or individuals and teacher directed; however, short whole-class activities were also planned such as use of a puppet who was 'learning to count' and made lots of mistakes for the children to point out. Modupe also committed to looking particularly for children counting during their child-initiated play activities during the week.

Tony would often ask Modupe informally how it was going and she grew in confidence as the children made progress and delighted in telling him how the children had come on. Six weeks later, similar assessment activities were repeated and progress noted.

Reflective task

Tony had to work harder than Emma on establishing a relationship with the professional learner. How successful do you think he has been in this? How does this coaching episode fit the GROW and Flow models of coaching? Thinking back to Rowland *et al.*'s (2009) knowledge quartet, which type of knowledge do you think Emma and Tony were trying to develop?

CONCLUSION

This chapter has introduced the ideas of leading professional development in mathematics in your school, centring on the concepts of mentoring and coaching as suggested by the Williams Review (2008). We have considered what mentoring and coaching are and, while acknowledging the varying definitions put forward by authors for this chapter, have decided that the role of the MaST fits best with specialist coaching (DfES 2005). Some approaches to coaching were outlined where the purposes of the coaching dictated the type of coaching that was appropriate. Two models of coaching were then considered; these were chosen as they were quite simple and easy to remember for teachers with busy lives including being a mathematics specialist. Readers were invited to consider their own principles for mentoring and coaching; the CUREE principles were offered for comparison purposes, however it was acknowledged that some people do not consider them to be principles, but rather statements for describing activities. Skills of coaching may overlap with skills of mentoring and mathematics specialists already possess many of these skills but may like to sharpen some of them in the development of their role. Various coaching activities were considered that could be used over time and in different contexts for developing the learning and teaching of primary mathematics across the school. Coaching is most effective in supportive environments and with supportive staff; we considered some of the barriers to that support and how they might be overcome. Use of collaboration was a theme here that was later explored through the second case study. In this chapter there was limited space for promoting other forms of professional development but we touched on this towards the end of the chapter and further reading is recommended in this area. The penultimate section discussed how coaching can actually become very helpful professional development for the coach as well as for the professional learner. The case studies asked you to apply your knowledge in considering different models of coaching and the different types of knowledge that were being promoted. We hope you enjoy working collaboratively to develop learning and teaching within your school.

FURTHER READING

Brockbank, A. and McGill, I. (2006) *Facilitating Reflective Learning through Mentoring and Coaching*. London: Kogan Page. A very comprehensive book about mentoring and coaching; reading this will assist in further understanding the differences between the two ideas and indeed the similarities. It will also provide much more detail on approaches and models that could be useful in coaching and mentoring.

Bubb, S. and Earley, P. (2010) *Helping Staff Develop in Schools*. London: Sage. This is a quick and easy, practical book that introduces the reader to a range of strategies to promote professional development in schools.

CHAPTER 6

CHAMPIONING THE TEACHING AND LEARNING OF MULTIPLICATION

INTRODUCTION

This chapter aims to develop your subject knowledge, pedagogical knowledge and skills of supporting colleagues in the area of multiplication by:

1   exploring mathematical connections between multiplication and other mathematical ideas and contexts and identifying the key ideas of multiplication;
2   considering aspects of using and applying knowledge and skills of multiplication;
3   identifying how children's learning of multiplication progresses through from the Early Years and into Key Stage 3;
4   identifying aspects of pedagogy designed to ensure children understand multiplication fully; including key aspects of multiplication to assess in children's learning, tasks which focus on using and applying and understanding multiplication, and effective resources and representations;
5   considering examples of how you can support your colleagues in this area.

This chapter is written to help you to support children in your school in having a relational understanding of multiplication. The term relational understanding was used by Skemp (1989). It implies having a full understanding of multiplication, being able to recognise it in a range of contexts, to work flexibly through different types of multiplication problems and to understand how to use a range of strategies of multiplication. Skemp contrasted this sort of understanding with instrumental understanding, which focuses more on memory of the procedures of multiplication. Of course you will want the children in your school to memorise multiplication facts and to calculate accurately. This chapter will consider how you can promote both recall of multiplication facts as well as a full understanding of multiplication as an operation.

DEEP SUBJECT KNOWLEDGE OF MULTIPLICATION

Mathematical connections

When we teach children about multiplication, we can draw on and make connections between other mathematical ideas they have already experienced, and a rich variety of real-life contexts which link to the operation. This section will consider some of these connections.

When they are too exposed to a diet of bare calculations such as $3 \times 4 = 12$, it can be difficult for older children in Key Stage 2 to recognise multiplication within a word problem. Writers such as Anghileri (2000) and Barmby *et al.* (2009) offer a discussion of the types of situations where multiplication arises. These include:

- ■ situations with equal groups of items or quantities, for example:
    - ■ How many children are needed for 6 five-a-side sports teams?
    - ■ What is the total amount in 3 tins of 0.5 litres of paint?
    - ■ How many tiles are needed for a rectangular array of 5 rows and 6 columns?
- ■ situations which involve a comparison, or scaling, or relationships such as ratios, for example:
    - ■ How many miles is a 5 km race?
    - ■ How much pocket money do you get if you get three times as much as your brother who gets £1.50?
- ■ situations which involve area or finding all possible combinations, for example:
    - ■ What is the total area of the classroom carpet measuring 2 m by 1.5 m?
    - ■ How many different sandwiches can you make if you choose one of brown bread or white bread, and one filling from cheese or ham?

In each case the numbers used in multiplicative problems may be whole numbers or numbers including fractions and refer to sets of objects or measures.

Reflective task

Consider the teaching and learning of mathematics in your school. Do you present children with a rich diet of situations to identify and explore multiplication, in order that they develop a full understanding of it?

What would each of these three situations look like in a reception class, a Year 3 class, a Year 6 class?

These situations help children to connect multiplication to real-life contexts and real-life contexts to their learning of multiplication in school, an important part of recognising multiplication in an investigation or word problem.

Reflective task

Consider the calculation 3 × 4 = 12.

Write down as many different ways of expressing this calculation as possible.

Say the calculation in as many different ways as you can.

Think of real-life contexts where this fact might occur.

Reflect on how many of your representations used the symbols or language of addition, or drew on repeated addition.

Multiplication has a deep connection to addition. The multiplication symbol can be thought of as shorthand for repeated addition, for example, 3 × 4 = 3 + 3 + 3 + 3. In this way, the symbol demonstrates a key feature of mathematics, the ability to express ideas in a very compact and abbreviated, shorthand manner. This is best shown where the repeated addition is itself rather tedious to write out in full.

Perhaps the strongest connection lies between multiplication and division, and in fact the operations are two sides of the same idea. You might have expressed the fact of 3 × 4 = 12 as a division, 12 divided by 3 is 4, or 12 divided by 4 is 3. An understanding of the relationship between multiplication and division enables children to have access to number facts readily, lessening the burden on their memory. In fact understanding that 3 × 4 = 12 gives access to the number facts:

12 / 3 = 4
12 / 4 = 3
120 / 30 = 4
120 / 40 = 3
120 / 3 = 40
120 / 4 = 30
1200 / 40 = 30, etc.

The link between multiplication and division can also underpin word problems which children meet. Children from the early years through to Year 6 can explore multiplication and division, their language and the connections between them in realistic contexts. In this way they will be able to use the language of both. For example they might discuss repeated addition of equal groups in multiplication and sharing or partitioning into equal groups in division.

Reflective task

Consider the problem:

> The class are all interested in collecting themed cards. The cards come in packs of six. How many packs would you need to buy to get 30 cards?

Would you consider this problem as using division or multiplication? Could children discuss the problem in terms of both operations? Could teaching one operation in isolation limit their understanding of the links?

Key mathematical ideas in multiplication

We have seen that multiplication connects closely to division and addition. In this section we will identify other key ideas relating to multiplication.

We have already seen that multiplication can be seen as repeated addition or repeated aggregation (Haylock 2010). Another key idea is that multiplication situations present one-to-many correspondences. One team represents 5 children, one kilometre is roughly $\frac{3}{5}$ miles, and one slice of brown bread could be paired up with two fillings. Nunes and Bryant (1996) call this the basis of multiplicative reasoning, which occurs before children learn about multiplication at school. Nunes *et al.* (2009) point out that children often use additive strategies to solve ratio problems such as: if 200 ml of white paint and 300 ml of blue paint mixed together provide a certain shade of colour, how much blue paint must be mixed with 500 ml of white paint to make the same shade? An over-reliance on additive reasoning can lead children to answer 600 ml rather than 750 ml. One explanation is that teachers and the curriculum focus on additive reasoning.

A further key feature of multiplication is that it is usually a binary operation. This is quite a complex idea but one which should add to your own subject knowledge of multiplication. Addition and subtraction are not binary operations. When we add and subtract, for example, the number of people sitting in a cafe, the numbers we deal with all refer to the same type of quantity, in this case the number of people. So that for a number sentence such as $24 + 8 = 32$ the 24 refers to the number of people already in the cafe when 8 people enter, making the total 32 people. Each number represents a total of people. This is not the case for a multiplication problem. Consider the problem: there are 6 people around each of 5 tables in the cafe, how many people are in the cafe? Here the 6 refers to the number of people around each table, the 5 to the number of tables occupied, and the 30 to the total number of people. The 6 (the multiplicand) and the 30 (the product) represent something different to the 5 (the multiplier).

The binary nature of multiplication connects it to some more complex compound contexts for the operation, such as the cost of petrol per litre or speed in miles per hour (Haylock and Cockburn 2008).

You may have noticed that when children solve a problem such as 3×6, they are performing a complex set of counting, relating to the binary nature of multiplication. They must count in 3s, unless they can remember the multiples of 3, while counting how many 3s they have counted, stopping when they complete 6 lots of 3, while keeping a running total.

For example, they must count:

1, 2, 3, one lot of three, 4, 5, 6, two lots of three, 7, 8, 9, three lots of three, 10, 11, 12, four lots of three, 13, 14, 15, five lots of three, 16, 17 18, six lots of three.

Each set of counting needs to be accurate and monitored carefully to reach the answer.

Therefore the binary nature of multiplication sets it apart from addition, although there are clear connections.

A further key feature of multiplication is that it is commutative, like addition, and different in this way to subtraction and division. Therefore $3 \times 4 = 4 \times 3$. This can be shown through situations and representations such as the ones we began with. In fact, for children to really understand that multiplication is commutative, an investigation of rich situations is key. For example, do 2 tins of three litres of paint really hold the same amount of paint as 3 tins of two litres of paint? Children may need to convince themselves of this.

Multiplication is also distributive over addition and subtraction. In other words:

$$a(b + c) = ab + ac$$
$$a(b - c) = ab - ac$$

Although we need not share this term with children, or this very formal recording, children will need to have this understanding to know that they can calculate 12×7 by adding 10×7 and 2×7, and we can calculate 18×7 by subtracting 2×7 from 20×7.

An ability to multiply provides children with the key skill of counting in steps other than 1. This is an extension from their first experiences of learning to count where they are required to match one item to one number name, called the one-to-one principle by Gelman and Gallistel (1978). Counting in 2s, or larger numbers, provides children with a more effective and efficient way of counting larger groups of items. They begin to manipulate numbers as objects themselves. Counting in 10s links directly to operations such as addition and subtraction. $47 + 36$ can then be calculated as $47 + 10 + 10 + 10 + 6$, a significantly quicker method than counting from 47 in 36 ones.

Multiplication also allows children to manipulate numbers by their factors. They can see 6 as two lots of 3. They can multiply numbers by using their factors, for example, 24×20 might be best calculated by $24 \times 2 \times 10$.

Multiplication is a complex operation, and the key ideas it relates to provide a rich area for investigation.

Using and applying multiplication

This section will consider using and applying activities which can involve children in deepening their understanding of multiplication.

Have a go at the following activities so that you can identify how they can add to children's understanding of contexts where multiplication might occur, the associated language and their understanding of multiplication itself.

Reflective task

How many different ice cream combinations can you make if you choose one of chocolate, strawberry or vanilla ice cream and one of a plain or almond cone? What if you choose one of two different sauces to go on top?

Party bags are made up each with three sweets, two stickers and four small toys. If 21 sweets are used, how many small toys will be needed?

When you count how many factors numbers have, which numbers have odd totals of factors?

How many squares are there on a chess board?

How did you use multiplication in your responses to these questions? Possible responses will be considered below.

Combinations and finding all possibilities investigations such as the ice cream task can be found in many forms. They might involve colouring flags of different stripes, designing football strips with coloured T-shirts, shorts and socks, making pizzas choosing from different sorts of toppings. They are useful to model to children how to list events methodically, ensuring that they have listed each once and only once. When children do so, they soon become aware of patterns in their results. For each type of ice cream, there will be two options of cones. If you choose from three types of ice cream and two cones, there will be 3×2 different ice cream combinations. If we add in a choice of two sauces, there will be $2 \times 3 \times 2$ options. Each sauce can be matched to six different ice cream combinations. Simple investigations of this sort, throughout children's primary education, increasing in the number of variables, can engage them in the language of pattern, multiplication and one-to-many relationships.

The party bag activity uses ideas of ratio, an example of a situation which is based on a multiplicative relationship. Sweets, stickers and toys are put into the party bags in the ratio of $3 : 2 : 4$. In order to solve this problem, we need to consider how many party bags can be filled with 21 sweets, and to then calculate how many toys are needed for this many party bags. Children are required to move between ideas of both multiplication and division.

When investigating how many factors different numbers have you will find that only square numbers have odd totals of factors. Factors usually come in pairs, $3 \times 5 = 15$, so 3 and 5 are factors of 15. Square numbers are unique in having a factor which does not have a 'partner': $3 \times 3 = 9$ so 3 is a factor of 9, with no 'partner' other than itself. Here children need to be able to recall number facts in order to explore properties of numbers. This adds to their number sense (Anghileri 2000).

When counting squares on an 8×8 chess board it should be possible to find:

One 8×8 square
Four 7×7 squares
Nine 6×6 squares
Sixteen 5×5 squares
Twenty-five 4×4 squares
Thirty-six 3×3 squares
Forty-nine 2×2 squares
Sixty-four 1×1 squares

making a total of 204 squares

Again this investigation should help children to begin to identify the square numbers with ease and confidence. In fact, it may be a source of wonder at the way this sequence of numbers crops up unexpectedly. They should identify the pattern both spatially as they identify the squares on the board and numerically.

Using and applying aspects of multiplication or identifying multiplication as they explore number puzzles and mathematics in contexts are key experiences for children. Multiplication is not just about rapid recall of number facts, however important these may be. Children need to understand when to multiply, what happens when they do multiply and to identify patterns of multiplication. This will allow them to work forwards and backwards through multiplication problems confidently, use multiplicative properties of numbers and identify the way multiplication occurs in nature, in real life and in many aspects of numbers.

Progression in children's understanding of multiplication

This section will explore how children's understanding of multiplication might progress from the Early Years Foundation Stage, and before, throughout Key Stage 1 and 2, into Key Stage 3. The aim is to give you an overview with which to critically consider progression of the children in your school.

Young children can experience ideas of multiplication before they come to school, in real contexts. For example, they might line up their toys in pairs to wait at a pretend bus stop, or seat them in rows to watch television, making a repeating addition pattern. They will come across real examples of arrays such as storing things in empty egg boxes, and of one-to-many relationships such as four toys sitting in each toy car. Barmby *et al.* (2009) and Nunes and Bryant (1996) claim that young children can understand this type of reasoning about one-to-many situations in meaningful contexts. Certainly very young children negotiate one-to-many situations, such as pairs of socks, fingers on a hand, etc. This sort of thinking is important to build on in school. Nunes *et al.* (2009) question the idea that children develop an understanding of addition and subtraction first, and that multiplication and division must develop later, building on these skills. Multiplicative reasoning begins early and should progress clearly through the primary curriculum.

This chapter has considered the experiences which children have before school which relate to multiplication. As they enter school, children should experience much more of this practical and contextual work on multiplication before the introduction of formal and abstract recording. As they progress through the primary phase, they will be required to solve more complex problems involving multiplication, so it seems sensible to continue this rich contextual work throughout, and avoid making multiplication a purely abstract idea.

These experiences should enable children to, for example:

- ■ replicate sets in meaningful contexts; for example saving up pocket money, or counting in steps such as 0.01;
- ■ talk about arrays, such as sets of windows in buildings, chunks in a bar of chocolate, egg boxes, rows of seats, collections of cards kept in albums, exploring the language of rows and columns, sets of, lots of, and the commutative and distributive laws;
- ■ experience situations with relationships such as working out the size of a giant from an enlarged photocopy of a hand span, or measuring the height of the classroom door, table and chairs, etc. and doubling them for a school for giants who are double the size of children;
- ■ explore situations such as working out how many different pairs can be made from a group of six children.

Reflective task

Do these experiences occur in all classes in your school?

What sort of multiplication experiences would you want to be taking place in a Year 2 class, a Year 4 class, a Year 6 class?

Can you ensure that the children in each year group experience situations of replication of equal groups, one-to-many correspondences, scaling and relationships such as doubling, and combination investigations?

Next we will consider progression in terms of the skills or strategies of multiplication, both mental and written. These can often progress through a series of steps which are outlined below. Progression in learning, however, is complex and children will not follow the steps steadily. These steps should only be seen as a guide which can help you to consider progression of children in your own class and across your own school. Some skills of multiplication take a long time, such as the rapid recall of number facts, and children will continue to learn these as they develop other skills. It is not necessary to stop tackling other areas until rapid recall is in place, although this is important in its own right.

- Rhythmic counting 1 2 **3** 4 5 **6** 7 8 **9** 10 11 **12** ….
- Doubling and halving
- Counting in 2s, 10s, 5s
- Counting in other steps 3, 4, 6, 7, 8, 9 etc., starting at zero and then from any number
- Recording of number facts, connecting multiplication and division, number triples such as 3, 4, 12
- Multiplying numbers by 10, 100 …
- Multiplying multiples of ten, e.g. 30×4, 3×40, 30×40
- Rapid recall of number facts
- Finding and exploring multiples of numbers
- Finding and exploring factors of numbers
- Using partitioning to multiply larger numbers, e.g. 12×3 as 10×3 and 2×3
- Multiplying mentally by using factors, or doubling one number and halving the other
- Informal written methods such as grid or area methods of multiplication
- Expanded short and long multiplication
- Compact short and long multiplication

Writers such as Anghileri (2000), Thompson (2010), Barmby *et al.* (2009), Nunes and Bryant (1996) have unpicked progression in detail.

As we have seen, multiplication is a rich operation which occurs in different situations, in differing ways. Although some parts of children's learning can be guided through a smooth progression, others are more complex. For example, mental methods of multiplication such as partitioning, as well as being invaluable in their own right, link well to the area method of multiplication. The area method of multiplication is a strong informal written method which provides a step towards children being able to multiply fractions, and algebraic equations, although it might not provide such as easy step to the formal written calculation. Consider the examples below.

6×23 can be worked out mentally as

6×20
6×3

This leads well to:

	20	3
6	120	18

which can then be recorded as:

```
  23
 ×6
 120   6 × 20
  18   6 × 3
 138
```

However, the compact form requires us to work from left to right and begin with 6×3 and to understand that this makes an extra ten which we need to add to 20×6.

```
  23
 ×6
 138
```

Here the progression is not so smooth. There are difficulties when moving from a mental or informal written method to the compact written method of multiplication, as in other operations. This is analysed in depth by Thompson (2010). The area method does, however, progress well to later learning such as:

$(x + 6) (y + 2)$

	y	2
x	xy	2x
6	6y	12

As a specialist teacher you can take an overview of progression through the school, to ensure that children deepen their understanding of multiplication in a rich range of situations. You will also want to ensure that children become increasingly precise and mathematical in their use of the language of multiplication. You will want children in your school to become more fluent and rapid in their recall of facts and also refine their mental and written strategies of calculation. Your awareness of the points where the progression may not run smoothly can help you to support your colleagues and provide written guidance on progression in calculations.

PEDAGOGICAL KNOWLEDGE

Knowledge of learners

This section considers the use of assessment to explore prior learning of multiplication, particularly their recall of table facts and an analysis of their errors.

Reflective task

What sort of knowledge of learners is necessary for the teachers in your school to ensure children progress in their understanding of multiplication?

We have already seen an argument that children learn about multiplicative thinking before they come to school, and that teachers should build on this from the reception year rather than seeing multiplication as a more difficult idea to be taught after an understanding of addition is in place. The next task provides an opportunity for you to consider the kind of activities that would enable teachers to explore children's existing understanding of multiplicative situations before they plan more formal work on multiplication.

Reflective task

Consider the activities below. How could they be used to assess previous learning? What sort of probing questions would you want teachers to ask to explore children's understanding?

When we play a game where pairs of matching cards are collected, shall we count the pairs or the cards to see who has won?

How many wellingtons in the cloakroom? How many pairs?

How could you arrange eight toys, making sure they sit in straight lines?

Describe the patterns of panes of glass in the windows.

Arrange the classroom chairs in lines for the class to watch a group of children performing some drama.

What are the common multiples of 2 and 3?

How would you work out how many cards you need to collect to fill a book with 32 pages, when each page has room for six rows of four cards?

If you wanted to arrange a number of counters in as many different rectangles as possible, what is a good number of counters to choose?

If I continue the sequence 1, 4, 7, 10 ... will I get to 300?

Children's rapid recall of number facts is a key area of multiplication to assess. The ability to memorise facts provides confidence and ease with mental and written methods of calculation. Your school may use regular tests to assess children's rapid recall of facts and to encourage them to practise them. Children may be expected to recite tables and answer facts at speed, but it will be as important to be fluent with table facts, to know facts out of order and when presented in different forms and language. Children with specific learning difficulties such as dyslexia may find this particularly difficult, and you will want to ensure that this does not become a barrier for them. Public competition in rapid recall of facts can encourage some but not all children. It might be more appropriate to play games in small groups where, for example, children multiply numbers perhaps as part of a board game with two dice. Children can keep a record on a multiplication table of the facts they know. They will then become aware of the patterns in the multiplication table. Table tests can take up a significant amount of lesson time and could be a lost opportunity if the focus is purely on getting an answer quickly. They then provide information about who can or cannot remember the facts, rather than giving any assessment information about how children calculate facts they cannot remember by rote. A test which includes rapid recall, but also other questions which require mental methods, followed by discussion of and sharing of these strategies, might be a better form of assessment. Knowledge of learners' ability to remember facts is crucial, but when teachers find out that children do not know certain facts, then teaching needs to be put in place to help them to do so, or to develop strategies to calculate answers, where they cannot be memorised.

As well as in this area of rapid recall of facts, teachers will also need to have knowledge of children's wider skills and understanding, such as their ability to:

■ consider 12 as 3×4 or 2×6 and to use this when it is helpful in calculations;
■ count in steps from any number, not just zero;
■ identify multiples of numbers on a 10×10 grid but also on a grid of any size. For example why do the multiples of 2 have a different pattern on a grid with nine squares across the top to one with ten squares across the top?
■ recognise and explore square numbers, visually, as number facts and as numbers themselves;
■ calculate factors of numbers;
■ explore prime numbers;
■ use and explore laws of divisibility.

These activities will demand recall of number facts but go beyond them to explore the number system and develop a relational understanding of multiplication.

Several writers, such as, more recently, Hansen (2011) and Thompson (2010), have recognised the importance of children's errors as a form of assessment of their learning. Teachers can often spot consistent errors in children's work, which suggest a misunderstanding or misconception rather than a slip in concentration or an occasional error. For example, a child may make consistent place value errors in a short multiplication, as below, or multiply a decimal number by ten by adding a zero to the end of it. Knowledge of learners can be increased by careful analysis of errors and mistakes.

Reflective task

Consider what this error tells you about the child's learning.

$$
\begin{array}{r}
12 \\
\times\,\underline{23} \\
36 \\
\underline{24} \\
\underline{60}
\end{array}
$$

As a specialist teacher you will be able to support teachers' knowledge of the children's learning of multiplication by ensuring that you and your colleagues take a full view of multiplication, valuing both rapid recall of facts and children's understanding of multiplication.

Task design

This section will challenge you to consider critically the tasks set for the children in your school.

Reflective task

Do tasks set by teachers in your school promote children's relational understanding of multiplication or their procedural understanding (Skemp 1989)? Do they challenge children to understand the ideas of multiplication as well as to calculate efficiently and accurately?

What sort of tasks promote children's relational understanding of multiplication? Consider these tasks:

- What happens when we multiply by 1?

  What happens when we multiply by 0?

  Convince someone else of your answer.

- Write a word problem which uses multiplication.

- What happens when you add three consecutive whole numbers?

These tasks are designed to address learning objectives relating to multiplication, but also to mathematical reasoning and other aspects of using and applying mathematics.

Tasks can ask children to practise rapid recall of number facts; others can ask children to focus on strategies for multiplication. Again this can be reflected in the learning objectives.

For example, you could set a task asking children to teach someone to calculate a very difficult table, such as the 17 times table. This difficult number opens up the need to discuss strategies for multiplication such as:

1×17 easy
2×17 double 17
3×17 double 17 and add one more 17
4×17 double and then double again
5×17 half 10×17
6×17 double 3×17 or add 17 to 5×17
7×17 double 17 and add it to 5×17
8×17 double, double, double
9×17 take 17 from 10×17
10×17 easy.

These strategies such as doubling and doubling again to multiply by 4 can be essential for children who cannot necessarily commit number facts to memory.

The multiplication square is full of patterns and an exploration of these patterns can make rich tasks which deepen children's understanding of multiplication. These connections are more important, claims Anghileri (2000), than memorising the facts themselves. For example:

■ Which multiplication tables have even answers?
■ Which multiplication tables have alternating odd and then even answers?
■ Which multiplication tables have patterns in the units digits of their answers?
■ Which multiplication tables have patterns when you add the units and tens digits in each answer?

Similarly, tasks which aim to focus on the pattern in the tables might require children to decode a table represented in letters.

Reflective task

Here is a multiplication table, not written in order, where the letters represent digits, but not necessarily in the order A = 1, B = 2.

Which multiplication table is it and which digit does each letter stand for?

A × G = DF
C × G = FD
D × G = G
B × G = DH
I × G = FC
DJ × G = GJ
G × G = I
H × G = FA
E × G = DE
F × G = B

Barmby *et al.* (2009) recommend tasks which ask children to discuss statements and convince others of whether they are always, sometimes or never true. For example, does multiplying make numbers bigger? Here children are encouraged to explain their reasoning, give examples and engage with general statements.

Reflective task

Challenge the teachers in your school to consider the tasks they set on multiplication. Do these focus on rapid recall and strategies for mental multiplication? Do they promote children's using and applying of multiplication? Do they call on realistic contexts for multiplication, reflecting equal addition, scaling and finding all combination situations? Do they require children to engage in the language of multiplication? Are contexts used alongside formal recording of multiplication, from the early years to Year 6?

The language of multiplication and the images used to teach it

This section will consider specifically some of the language of multiplication, and evaluate some of the images commonly used to teach children to understand multiplication.

Learning about multiplication requires children to explore commutativity, the link between division and multiplication, and the associated language. For example, a range of language could be used to explain the meaning of $3 \times 4 = 12$:

3 lots of 4 are the same as 12
4 lots of 3 are the same as 12

3 groups of 4 are 12

4 groups of 3 are 12

3 multiplied by 4 is the same as 12

3 times 4 is 12

This raises the question of whether 3 groups of 4 means the same as 3 multiplied by 4 and as a consequence whether they should both be represented by the same image. If we use the language 3 groups of 4, we use an image showing a group of four things replicated three times. The language '3 multiplied by 4' should be demonstrated by a group of three things replicated four times. The number sentence 3 × 4 means a group of three things, replicated four times. However, the key idea is that these give the same answer.

The task of filling in the missing numbers reveals a number of interesting points. For example, 3 × 4 = ?. Any of the language above would help the children find the solution. They might think about how many is 3 lots of 4 or 3 groups of 4, and count in 4s. They might consider what is 3 multiplied by 4 and count in 3s.

The problem 3 × ? = 12 is harder to solve if children use the language three lots of what number is the same as 12? Unless they understand the commutative rule can be used for multiplication, this language is not helpful and suggests a trial-and-error method. Could it be three lots of two? Three lots of five? It would be better to think 3 multiplied by what number is 12, and count up in 3s.

However, the problem ? × 4 = 12 is not best solved by thinking which number multiplied by 4 is 12. Here the language 'how many groups of 4 is 12' does provide a way to find the solution, by counting in 4s.

The probems 3 × ? = 12 and ? × 4 = 12 are significantly different, requiring different ways of thinking about multiplication and different language, unless we use the commutative law. Children will need to consider the connections between the different ways we can talk about multiplication.

Haylock and Cockburn (2008) suggest that children should not record multiplication formally until they have understood the commutative nature of multiplication. This would certainly help children to tackle both calculations. However, even when they do grasp the commutative law, they will still need to use both the language and images of 'lots of' and 'multiplied by'.

As the specialist maths teacher in your school, you will want to ensure that the images for multiplication used, particularly with young children, support them as they progress through Key Stages 1 and 2 and into Key Stage 3. Some images are argued to be more effective in supporting progression than others.

This chapter has already identified the situations where multiplication arises. These can be represented in different ways. These representations might be practical with objects, drawn as jottings or pictures or manipulated in the mind. Here we will discuss three types, some of which we have referred to earlier. The references are to our first examples of situations where multiplication occurs:

■   First, we can represent multiplication as repeated addition. For example, we can solve the first problem of the number of children needed for 6 five-a-side teams by adding groups of five children. This could be modelled practically with real children, or cubes or pictures to represent children, or on an empty number line, for example. This representation works well with a whole number of groups and items within a group.

■ We can also represent multiplication as a one-to-many correspondence, perhaps represented as a mapping with arrows (Anghileri 2000).

■ Multiplication can be represented as a rectangular array of items, such as an egg box with two rows of three eggs. We might draw the carpet to scale to find its area, or show the combinations of different sorts of sandwiches as a table. The number of children in each five-a-side team can be drawn in a row, with more rows added for extra teams. This representation demonstrates the structure of multiplication, in its regularity of rows and columns.

Reflective task

Are these representations used in your school and the key ideas they demonstrate discussed with children?

Barmby *et al.* (2009) provide a convincing argument that the array is the most effective representation of multiplication. By providing a uniform display of objects in row and columns, the array exposes the key ideas of replication of equal groups, the commutative law and the fact that multiplication is distributive over addition. The image provides support in progression for children moving from the partitioning mental method to the written area method. Other images such as repeated addition of items might make replication of equal groups clear, but when the items are arranged randomly, the commutative and distributive law are not well demonstrated. The array therefore is a better image to support children's calculation and progression in their learning.

Good subject knowledge should underpin your use of images and language, and your support for your colleagues in this area. This includes considering the later learning the children will encounter and judging how best to support them for that.

COACHING AND MENTORING SCENARIOS

Use the arguments considered in this chapter to think about how you might support and challenge colleagues in these scenarios. What sort of good practice would you want to share from your own classroom? What arguments might you put forward?

What literature could you call on? Would written guidance help to support them? Which mentoring or coaching strategies might be most appropriate?

Scenario 1

An experienced colleague uses table tests every week to encourage children to learn the table facts. This is well received by most parents and the children are making good progress in their rapid recall. However, a small number of children are becoming very anxious about the tests and their confidence in mathematics generally has dipped. The teacher is concerned about these children and how to help them without dropping the high expectations of the whole class.

Scenario 2

You notice in your book scrutiny that much of one year groups' work on multiplication is very abstract. The teachers in that team report that this is because the children find reading word problems difficult.

Scenario 3

Your head teacher asks you to lead a Key Stage 2 staff meeting on analysing errors in children's written methods for multiplication. This is because the head is concerned that children do not appear to understand the methods when questioned during lesson observations.

CONCLUSIONS

This chapter aimed to help you to consider how the children in your school can become proficient in the skills of multiplication and reach a full understanding of the operation. It has considered how your deep subject knowledge and critical consideration of the teaching and learning of multiplication can promote children's relational understanding. Rapid recall of facts is a key area, and skills of accurate multiplication are essential, but multiplication offers more than this. Multiplication is a complex operation, but it is one which is found in many real-life situations and it offers a wealth of patterns and connections which can fascinate children.

FURTHER READING

Nunes, T. and Bryant, P. (1996) *Children Doing Mathematics*. Oxford: Blackwell Publishers. This book provides a detailed look at the structures of multiplication and children's progression in understanding them.

Nunes, T., Bryant, P. and Watson, A. (2009) *Key Understandings in Mathematics*. London: Nuffield Foundation. This document brings together a range of research findings.

Barmby, P., Bilsborough, L., Harries, T. and Higgins, S. (2009) *Primary Mathematics: Teaching for Understanding.* Maidenhead: OUP. This book argues in detail for the use of the array as the image for multiplication.

Thompson, I. (2010) 'Progression in the teaching of multiplication', in I. Thompson (ed.) *Issues in Teaching Numeracy in Primary Schools.* Maidenhead: OUP. This chapter looks critically at progression in children's understanding of written methods of multiplication.

CHAPTER 7

CHAMPIONING THE TEACHING AND LEARNING OF TIME

INTRODUCTION

This chapter aims to explore the features of 'deep subject knowledge' and 'pedagogical knowledge' in the context of time, to support your work with children and colleagues. Within the subject knowledge section key mathematical ideas will be identified, followed by a consideration of progression within time. Connections to other mathematical ideas and aspects of using and applying mathematics will be discussed. Finally, the pedagogy section will explore classroom applications, followed by scenarios for mentoring and coaching.

DEEP SUBJECT KNOWLEDGE OF TIME

Identifying key mathematical ideas

The principles involved in understanding time may be difficult to appreciate at first glance. For example, the passage of time can be subjective, depending on whether we are doing something pleasant, such as watching a favourite TV programme, or potentially unpleasant like waiting during a hospital appointment! Also, we experience the passage of time differently as we get older and with hindsight – how long does yesterday seem to you compared with the whole of last week?

Children also experience time differently; the more events that occur the shorter, or longer, the time scale can appear depending on the nature of the events. Then we have differing scales of time, e.g. computers work in microseconds or nanoseconds, historical time occurs over decades, centuries and millennia, while geological time is measured in millions and billions of years.

From these points it can be seen that the teaching of time is no simple matter and yet it is rewarding to realise that for the majority of people telling the time and working with time is second nature, so as teachers we must be doing something right!

The key ideas involved in understanding time can be summarised as:

1   the sequencing of events;
2   the 'passing' of time including concepts of the present, past and future and vocabulary such as before, after, now, has happened or will happen;
3   relating the passage of time to oneself and others, such as 'I came to school today' or 'I had a birthday party yesterday';
4   reading time, telling the time of day using analogue and digital clocks. Also, estimating time and knowing the difference in meaning between such phrases as 'I'll be with you in a minute' and 'the train leaves in one minute';
5   understanding and applying the units of time from seconds, minutes, hours, days, weeks, years, etc. to reading time and understanding duration, working with 60 seconds for 1 minute and 60 minutes in 1 hour. (The reason for working with 60 goes back to the Babylonians, who counted in base 60);
6   calculations involving time and time scales, such as using timetables, time zones nationally and across the world, including the International Date Line, Greenwich Mean Time, British Summer Time, etc. (Times across the UK were only standardised in November 1840 due to the railways, similarly in the 1850s in the USA. Imagine what it would be like to teach using non-standardised timetables!)

These key points are not linear although there is an overall hierarchy, for example being able to read and record the time of day is clearly a precursor to calculating journey durations or finding equivalent times across the world. There are links between the key ideas which will be explored below. For now, we will develop a workable progression of the ideas for teaching purposes.

Tracing mathematical progression

Based on the work of Duncan (1996), Biggs and Sutton (1983), the Primary National Strategy (DfES 2006) and other general reading, a workable progression is:

■   ordering events from the children's everyday lives;
■   use terms such as long time, short time, before, after, next, day, night, young, old, age, past, present, future, etc. in classroom conversations;
■   use the days of the week in everyday contexts;
■   during the school day use the vocabulary associated with units of time in an informal manner especially minutes and hours, reading from a 12-hour digital and analogue clock;
■   gain some insight into the duration of a minute and an hour;
■   begin to know the days of the week in sequence;
■   begin to know the seasons and months of the year;
■   relate the passage of time over a day to the hours and position of the sun;
■   read the hour on an analogue clock face and equate to a 12-hour digital clock;

- read the half and quarter hours on a clock face and equate to a 12-hour digital clock;
- speak and write the time for whole, half and quarter hours from a clock face and 12-hour digital readout and link them together, including understanding the recording of time as 9:30;
- be able to read the time to five minutes and speak it, including aspects such as '20 past 9' and '20 to 10';
- begin to understand the relationship between units of time such as 60 seconds make 1 minute, 60 minutes make 1 hour and 24 hours make 1 day. Use vocabulary such as dawn and dusk, midnight, midday;
- order the days in a week and know there are about 30 days in a month and 12 months in a year. Use vocabulary such as weekend, hourly, daily, weekly or monthly cycle;
- begin to order the months of the year and relate them to a calendar and the seasons;
- know and work with dates such as birthdays, school holidays, etc.;
- estimate and use suitable units of time from seconds to years related to the duration of events in their own lives;
- read and record time to the nearest minute and equate times from an analogue and a 12-hour digital clock;
- understand and use am and pm;
- understand and use 24-hour clock notation, including equating day, night, am, pm, analogue and 24-hour digital clock times;
- begin to use timetables to plan journeys;
- calculate straightforward durations using minutes and hours, such as journey times;
- calculate durations such as journey times using minutes and hours, extending to include days and seconds;
- work effectively using the different time zones across the world;
- relate time taken to complete a task to vocabulary such as speed and velocity.

As for the key points above, the progression is not linear, although there is again an overall hierarchy; for example some children will be able to order months of the year but still have difficulty in reading the time on a clock face. Others may be able to calculate effectively with digital time but have great difficulty relating digital time to a clock face.

We shall now briefly explore some of the above more fully, along with some activities which will aim to extend our thinking about time.

Reflective task

Without referring to any published source, make a list of all the words you can think of associated with time. Include everything such as 'period, time scale, century' etc; some of them are in the progression above. You may be surprised at the length of the list, which illustrates how complex time is as a topic for teaching!

Now try to order the list according to the progression above and your knowledge of working with children.

What difficulties did you find in doing this? Are there any aspects of your own subject knowledge which you now need to develop regarding the teaching of time?

Making mathematical connections

As discussed in Chapter 2, we can now consider connections across the mathematics and wider primary curriculum to enhance insight into our subject knowledge regarding time as a topic. To achieve this we will consider exemplars from the progression points above and consider links across the curriculum (see Table 7.1).

The above ideas are only intended as starters for discussion which need much refinement, but they do illustrate the range of possibilities involved.

Reflective task

Take one of the progression points above and discuss with colleagues how you could develop a teaching programme involving other aspects of mathematics and cross-curricular links. What activities could you use? What resources would you need? If possible try out your ideas on a small scale and bring the results back for a further discussion with colleagues. What have you learned about your teaching and the children's learning regarding time?

Using and applying

As considered in Chapter 2, it is important for children to develop their investigation and problem-solving skills so that they can apply their knowledge and understanding to explore mathematical ideas and challenges of the 'real' world. Skemp (1989) refers to instrumental and relational learning, the former focusing mainly on skills development while the latter involves greater understanding of the content related to other ideas in mathematics and wider learning. Nunes *et al.* (2009) refer to the importance of children developing a connection between quantity and number but also being able to distinguish between them. Fairclough in Koshy and Murray (2002) explores aspects of skills development through problem solving. In developing these ideas the topic of time lends itself well to investigative work and real-world application, as well as the need for skills development.

■ **Table 7.1** Illustrative links between progression in time and the mathematics curriculum

Progression points	Illustrative links to mathematics	Possible links to the wider curriculum
Ordering events from the children's everyday lives	Ordering numbers; sorting properties for similar and dissimilar events such as attending school, birthdays	Ordering a historical number line for recent events
Use the days of the week in everyday contexts	Counting objects, representing days of the week by icons. Counting on and back	Link to children's birthday and citizenship, sharing and giving
Relate the passage of time over a day to the hours and position of the sun	Link to other aspects of measure such as length of shadows, standard units of measure	Aspects of science, warmth, heat, cold, temperature, weather, stars
Be able to read the time to five minutes and speak it, including aspects such as '20 past 9' and '20 to 10'	Estimation of quantities, accuracy and precision in measures. Calculations involving difference between numbers	Use of clocks to time experiments in science, development of clocks in history
Understand and use 24-hour clock notation, including equating day, night, am, pm, analogue and 24-hour digital clock times	Calculations in base 60, angles between hands on an analogue clock	Travel times in geography, historical use of 24-hour clock
Calculate durations such as journey times using minutes and hours, extending to include days and seconds	Calculations involving different bases, money, planning an efficient sequence for visits, use of ICT	Times and timing in music, local and national journeys in geography

Some examples are given below:

1   How long is a second, minute? What can you do in 30 seconds, a minute, two minutes …?
2   Use tockers, sand timers, water clock, sundial, etc. to measure lengths of time.
3   How accurately can you measure time using a sundial, kitchen clock …?
4   Provide a timetable for your school day. How long are lessons, assembly, lunchtime, etc.?
5   What is the difference in age between the youngest and oldest in the class?
6   How many years, months, days, etc. have you been alive?
7   What is the length of time you spend in school and at home over a day, week …?
8   Compare the length of time you are awake and asleep over a week, month, year …

9   How long does it take to walk, jog or run 100 metres?

10   What are the record times for Olympics events? Do you have a 'feel' for how fast these are?

11   Use a TV programme guide to explore the lengths of programmes, compare the amount of time spent on sport, drama, etc. (This would link well with data handling.)

12   Why are there 30 days in some months and 31 in others? What is a leap year and why do we have them? How much longer is a leap year in seconds than an 'ordinary' year?

13   How do you calculate the age of someone born on 29 February?

14   Use local bus or rail timetables to plan journeys and calculate lengths of time.

15   Plan a holiday taking into account travel between different time zones.

16   Why is the International Date Line called that? What does it mean? What happens if you fly across it, do you lose a day, gain a day or stay the same?

17   How fast do you walk at a normal pace?

18   How do we know that the dinosaurs existed about 200 million years ago? Did someone measure this time?

19   Use analogue clocks, am, pm, 12- and 24-hour digital clocks to equate times.

20   If a clock gains five minutes every hour when will it be showing the correct time again if it's correct at 1 pm?

21   Are you actually older than your birthday indicates if last year was a leap year?

22   What do we mean when we say that a computer carries out calculations in nanoseconds?

23   Use a calendar to pose questions of time lengths, patterns such as number of weeks in a lunar cycle, etc.

24   What day was it on 1 January 2010, 1 January 1910, etc.?

25   Explore the cycles of time for festivals, etc. How long do aspects of a festival last? Why?

As can be seen, there are many situations which we can use from the child's everyday experiences which can be the basis for exploration regarding using and applying.

Reflective task

Consider how time is presently taught in your school. Is it presented mainly as a skills development activity, as in reading the time, or does it include aspects of using and applying as a matter of course? What resources, equipment, schemes of work, etc. are used? What are the good points regarding children's learning of time? How could it be improved? What do you need to do to begin that improvement?

There are many cross-curricular possibilities for exploring time, for example:

1   How did the Romans or Victorians read the time?
2   What is the importance of keeping time in music?
3   Carry out speed measures in science, or how long a bulb can last, or how long it takes a plant to grow.
4   How is time represented in literature? What words convey a sense of time such as rush, listless, pacing, running, headlong?
5   Use of time zones across the world in geography.
6   The importance of accurate time measurements in sport.
7   How do other languages structure the reading of time?
8   How can the passage of time be depicted through artwork? How has art changed through time?

Reflective task

What cross-curricular work is carried out in your classroom and school? What links are made regarding time as a topic to other subjects or aspects of the curriculum? How can the teaching of time be enhanced through such project work? What would you need to do to help develop such an approach?

PEDAGOGICAL KNOWLEDGE

Knowledge of learners

This section explores the use of assessment in gaining insight into prior knowledge regarding time, including consideration of possible errors and misconceptions.

Most children will come to school with some idea of time, for example through everyday use of time vocabulary by adults, the celebration of birthdays and festivals and names of the seasons. They will also have direct experience of sequencing events such as having to get out of bed and getting dressed before coming to school! However, it is unlikely that these ideas will have been explored in any systematic fashion. It is important that the skill level and understanding of children is assessed so that planning can focus on suitable differentiation of tasks for groups and individuals in the classroom. Gaining a rounded assessment of a child's understanding can be lengthy, but strategies to carry out this process include:

■   Talking to the children about their experiences related to their day, week, holidays, birthdays, etc. and listening to their responses. Discussion and questioning can then take place related to the progression of ideas discussed earlier. For example, we can consider a form of two-stage questioning aimed at eliciting reasoning as follows, 'What time did we start school, lesson … this morning? Can you explain to me how you know the start time?'

■ Working alongside the children on time tasks and activities, seeing what they can do and asking questions to gain insight into their thinking, e.g. what makes you think that the hands on the clock are in that position for 9 am? Where would they be at 9:05? Why is that?

■ Providing a range of activities for children including explorative and practical work so that a teacher can gain insight into reasoning through observation and discussion.

■ Marking children's work, paying attention to any pointers as to their thinking, not just 'getting the right answer'.

■ Listening to children working in groups or pairs where one is explaining the mathematics involved in a time task to others. Ask the others to explain to you what is going on and why.

■ Asking individuals to explain their mathematics to the class, as long as you know that they can cope with being put on the spot. Pick out the vocabulary that they use so that you can gauge understanding and refine their vocabulary later.

■ Using informal talk in the classroom to help foster time concepts such as 'Is it nearly lunchtime yet? How long is left to go?'

Reflective task

Consider what questions and contexts you could use to develop suitable aspects of time with your class on an informal and formal basis. How does this compare with your previous teaching of time? Are there any points or strategies you can develop further? How? Are there any aspects you can develop with colleagues?

Any knowledge of learners also needs to include the types of errors and misconceptions they may have regarding the study and understanding of time. Common errors include:

■ misinterpreting the order of events for individuals, e.g. some children may have school lunch and go out to play, while others may play first then have lunch;

■ counting on incorrectly so that three days from Tuesday is Friday, not Thursday!

■ mistaking the hour and minute hands when using an analogue clock;

■ confusing the different ways we tell the time so that 9:15 is 'quarter past 9' or 'fifteen minutes past 9' or '3 past 9'. 9:45 is 'three quarters past 9' or '45 minutes past 9' or '9 past 9'. 'Half past 9' becomes '30 past 9' or '6 past 9'. Also, 9:15 can be read as '15 to 9'!

■ misinterpreting digital clocks as decimal so 10:30 is seen as '10.3';

■ using 100 minutes in an hour instead of 60 when carrying out calculations, e.g. 3.5 hours becomes 3 hours 50 minutes;

■ confusion between the number of days in a lunar month and a calendar month. What happens to 29 February? Why?

■ moving from a 24-hour clock to am and pm so 01.15 is seen as 1.15 pm.

Reflective task

Work with colleagues to make a list of specific errors or misconceptions you have come across when teaching time. How did you overcome these or use the actual misconception to help your teaching? What resources did you need or would have helped?

A child tells you her favourite television programme starts at 6:00 and lasts for half an hour so finishes at 6:50. How would you confirm that you have correctly identified the misconception and teach to overcome this?

Task design

Consider what we mean by task design in teaching the topic of time. There are clear skills that need development, such as reading time from an analogue clock. However, since we rely on the measuring of time so much in our everyday lives, we need to address the children's understanding of time in different contexts as well as developing their skills.

We have already discussed the extensive vocabulary of time, along with the range of concepts involved. These will only have meaning for the children initially based on their everyday lives and increasingly extending outside their immediate experience.

Consider the following tasks:

Task 1
School starts at 9 o'clock and the first lesson lasts for 50 minutes. At what time does the lesson finish? Use a clock face to help you.

Lunchtime finishes at 1:00 pm and starts 50 minutes earlier. What time does lunchtime start?

Task 2
What time do you start school? Can you show this on a clock and write down the digital time? Write down the times for lessons during the morning. How long does each lesson last? Which is the longest lesson or are they all the same

length of time? How many minutes do you have for break? Which seems longer, a lesson or break? Why?

Do you spend more time on lessons in the morning or the afternoon? How much longer or shorter is the afternoon?

The first task focuses exclusively on skills development as it stands, although it can be extended and developed through good teaching. The second approach attempts to contextualise the work based on the children's experiences, and so making it more real. It is also easily extendable or can be cut back depending on the children's previous experiences and understanding. Using discussion in the second task can also help learners to provide reasons for their ideas and so develop deeper thinking skills. The use of prediction and hypothesising can also bring the activity more alive, for example 'Which do you think is the longest, the time you spend in school in the morning or afternoon?' This allows children to estimate and then to explore the solution more precisely.

A blend of skills development and problem-solving work is required to aid understanding, although skills can be developed by learners through the solution of suitable problems. These can also provide a context and a strong reason for the development of the skills.

Reflective task

Which do you think is the longest, the number of seconds in a minute or the number of minutes in a day? Do you have to do an actual calculation? How many minutes are there to the end of today? (Health warning, a calculator may be useful here!)

Choose an aspect of time that you intend to teach from the progression above. Find or design a closed, skills-focused question associated with that aspect of time, possibly linked to the cross-curricular ideas above. Develop this into a wider activity based on the children's previous mathematical and everyday experiences. Try both approaches in the classroom. Analyse what went well and not so well. What was the impact on children's learning? How would you explain your findings to a colleague who is concerned about teaching that aspect of time? What have you learned from the exercise?

From the discussion above we can see that the assessment of children's knowledge linked to a range of appropriate tasks and activities, initially based on their everyday experiences, is key to developing understanding as well as skills.

A final thought for us: if children enjoy finding out about dinosaurs how can we harness that to teach concepts of time involving millions of years, which is outside their normal experience?

COACHING AND MENTORING SCENARIOS

This section deals with working alongside colleagues in helping them to further develop their teaching skills, now that we have considered subject and pedagogical knowledge regarding time. The scenarios below are intended to be progressive, working from your own class to helping across the whole school. Discuss the situations with colleagues on the MaST programme and prepare strategies to deal with the situations. You could also use the scenarios in your own school to help development if appropriate.

Scenario 1

You have been approached by an NQT in your school who is concerned about teaching time to her Year 3 class. She is intending to work on telling the time in minutes and hours but is unsure how to set about it. Unfortunately during her training she never had the opportunity to teach time as a topic. She has heard that it's good to use clock faces for practical work and she is adept at using the IWB. They are doing a project on the ancient Egyptians and she thinks she would like to link the mathematics to the project. How would you advise her to proceed? How could you help, would you need further resources or support? Are there any aspects of your own knowledge that you need to develop?

Scenario 2

The Year 6 team of three teachers is introducing work on time zones across the world. They want you to lead a team-teaching lesson for an hour to start the week's work and would also like you to give them activities for the remainder of the week since you're the MaST expert! The head teacher has agreed to release you to do the introductory lesson.

How will you set about working with the Year 6 team, bearing in mind that your task is to develop their teaching as well as the children's learning?

Scenario 3

Analysis of SAT-type questions has shown that children do not perform well at the end of Key Stage 1 or 2 when answering questions on time. The head teacher wants you to run a staff meeting for an hour to develop teachers' understanding of the teaching of time from Reception to Year 6. How will you set about this? What can you realistically achieve and what support do you need to enable the staff meeting and subsequent developments to be a success?

CONCLUSION

In this chapter we set out to explore aspects of subject and pedagogic knowledge associated with the topic of time. We have seen the range of concepts involved and the complexity of the passage of time and its measurement. Several ideas have been considered to enhance the teaching and learning of time concepts. Since time is such an essential part of our lives it is important that children understand its nature and can apply their skills and reasoning to solve problems. The wealth of situations regarding time can itself be a rich source of activities and ideas for working with children and can help motivate their learning. Although complex, the enjoyment associated with taking part in a child's developing understanding of time is without equal; enjoy your teaching!

FURTHER READING

Duncan, A. (1996) *What Primary Teachers Should Know About Maths*. 2nd edn. London: Hodder and Stoughton. This book encapsulates key points regarding time and its learning.

Biggs, E. and Sutton, J. (1983) *Teaching Mathematics 5 to 9*. London: McGraw-Hill. Chapter 16 provides some useful insights into time activities in the classroom.

Cotton, T. (2010) *Understanding and Teaching Primary Mathematics*. Essex: Pearson Education Limited. This is a good overall reference including discussion of some specific misconceptions.

 CHAPTER **8**

CHAMPIONING THE TEACHING AND LEARNING OF DATA HANDLING

INTRODUCTION

This chapter aims to consider the features of 'deep subject knowledge' and 'pedagogical knowledge' in the context of data handling by:

- exploring the key features of data handling;
- identifying how children's learning develops through from the early years into Key Stage 3;
- considering links between models of problem solving and the data handling cycle;
- identifying aspects of pedagogy designed to allow children to explore all aspects of data handling;
- considering coaching and mentoring scenarios.

This chapter is written to help you to support children in your school in developing a full understanding of the nature of data handling. It is also designed to support your work with other teachers in developing a deep understanding of each of the features of subject knowledge and making informed pedagogical choices.

For the purposes of this chapter the term data handling will be used to refer to the processes that are involved in addressing questions that can be answered by collecting information (data that might be collected in answering questions of measures of chance or probability is not considered in this chapter).

DEEP SUBJECT KNOWLEDGE OF DATA HANDLING

Price and Raker (2003) considered teachers' confidence in teaching data handling. They found that teachers' subject knowledge in data handling was a substantial issue. They go on to suggest that the reason for this lack of confidence could be lack of appropriate training.

Identifying key mathematical ideas

In Chapter 2 we put forward the argument that deep subject knowledge includes the ability to identify the key mathematical ideas in a topic, lesson or activity, rather than those on the periphery. In this section we identify an initial list of key ideas and then further consider the potential for peripheral aspects of those key themes to be given greater focus in schools.

One way of expressing the key ideas in data handling is to consider the stages in the data handling process:

1   *Specify the problem.* This could include formulating questions or deciding who might want to know the answer and why.
2   *Planning for data collection.* At this stage children would be involved in deciding what information to collect, the sample size needed, the format for data collection and so on.
3   *Gathering data.* This can include both primary sources such as experiments and surveys and the interrogation of secondary sources such as data bases.
4   *Representing data.* Children would need to choose an appropriate form of representation to reflect the kind of data collected and the nature of the question posed.
5   *Interpreting data.* At this stage children will be engaged in using the data to answer the original question posed.

These ideas can also be presented in diagrammatic form in order to indicate the cyclical nature of the data handling process and to draw children's attention to the aspect of the data handling cycle that they are focusing on. See Figure 8.1.

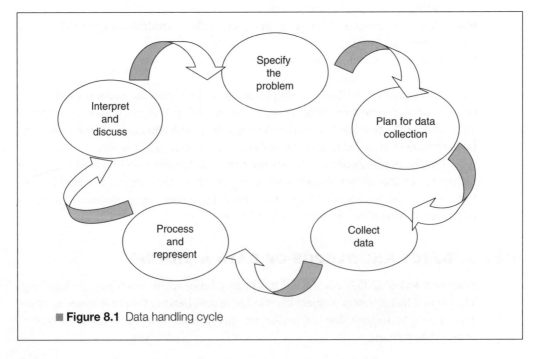

■ **Figure 8.1** Data handling cycle

There has been a suggestion (for example from QCA and the NNS) that there has been an overemphasis on the collection and representation of data and that because too little time is spent on the planning and interpretation phases, data handling lessons can become 'aimless'. A typical scenario would be a group of children wandering around school 'doing a survey' for no apparent reason. This would then be followed by time spent 'colouring in' various graphical representations. It could therefore be argued that peripheral aspects of the data handling cycle to do with data collection and representation take up too much time in mathematics lessons.

Reflective task

Consider the teaching and learning of data handling in your own school. Is there an overemphasis on data collection? Do activities lack a clear purpose? Is too much time spent on presentation?

Another key mathematical idea is that there are differences in nature of the data that is collected. Broadly speaking, data sources can be divided into two different types: data that is counted and data that is measured.

Data that is counted includes:

■ *Categorical data.* Categorical data cannot be ordered, for example pets, hobbies, flavours of crisps and so on.
■ *Discrete data.* Discrete data is defined as numerical data which has no intermediate for example shoe size, house numbers and test scores.

Data that is measured includes:

■ *Continuous data.* The key feature here is that intermediate points do have value, for example height, temperature, time and so on.

It is important for children to understand the difference between discrete and continuous data as this will influence approaches to the collection of data (and so must be considered at the planning stage) and because discrete and continuous data may be represented in different ways.

Making mathematical connections

In Chapter 2 we suggested that a key component of deep subject knowledge was a knowledge, understanding and awareness of conceptual connections within and between the areas of primary mathematics curriculum.

The connectedness of the stages of the data handling cycle becomes evident as soon as the problem or question is posed. The context, nature and number of questions posed will affect what data will need to be collected, the choice of presentation and the tools used for analysis. For example, the nature of the data collected and the representation of that data will be very different for the two questions listed below:

■ Which cafe sells the cheapest sandwiches?
■ Which cafe sells the healthiest sandwiches?

Connections can also be made with other aspects of mathematics. Forms of representation which are used for sorting (tables, Carroll diagrams and Venn diagrams) can also be used to sort shapes and numbers in order to reveal relationships and make generalisations. For example, by sorting multiples of 2 and multiples of 4 using a Venn diagram it becomes clear that multiples of 4 are also multiples of 2. Or by sorting triangles children may realise that right-angled triangles can be either scalene or isosceles but not equilateral. Further links could be made with shape (angle) and with number (percentages) when children are required to construct a pie chart.

Reflective task

Consider the extent to which you use aspects of the data handling cycle to make links with other aspects of the mathematics curriculum; for example to explore properties of shape or number.

Tracing mathematical progression

As the discussion above indicates, the key stages in the data handling cycle are non-hierarchical and run in parallel. Thus a child in a Reception class would be expected to engage with all five aspects of the data handling cycle and so would a child in Year 6. However, it is the nature of that engagement with each of the key ideas that develops over time. Thus there is progression both within and across each of the five stages of the data handling cycle, which will be considered in further detail in the following sections, starting with progression in representation.

Progression in representation
Analysis of various curriculum documents (NNS, PNS, National Curriculum) reveals that primary children may encounter graphical representations in the following order:

■ lists and tables
■ Carroll diagrams
■ Venn diagrams
■ pictograms
■ block graphs
■ bar charts

- ■ line graphs
- ■ pie charts
- ■ scatter graphs.

Complexities in identifying a straightforward linear progression in representation of data are revealed when we consider the potential for different graphical representations to show the same data. For example, both a Venn diagram and a Carroll diagram could be used to sort odd numbers and multiples of 3 (see Figures 8.2 and 8.3).

This then raises the question of whether the list above, which suggests that Carroll diagrams are more complex than Venn diagrams, is in fact correct. The task below invites you to consider if the same can be said for bar charts and pie charts, for example.

There is also progression within each of the forms of representation. Carroll diagrams can be used to sort data according to a single criterion (for example, has blue eyes or does not have blue eyes). This can then be extended to a second criterion (for example, has blue eyes and wears glasses). Similarly, according to the question posed and the data set involved, Venn diagrams can be constructed from either two or three rings. When using pictograms a level of difficulty is added if the picture represents more than one piece of data. For bar charts the level of complexity is increased as the scale on the vertical axis changes and line graphs could extend to any number of lines on a single set of axes.

To summarise, when considering progression in representation we need to take into account that identifying a clear progression in representation of data is complex because:

- ■ different graphs can show the same data set
- ■ there is progression within each form of representation.

	Odd	Not odd
Multiple of 3	3 9 15 21 27	6 12 18 24 30
Not a multiple of 3	1 5 7 11 13 17 19 23 25 29	2 4 8 10 14 16 20 22 26 28

■ **Figure 8.2** Carroll diagram used to sort odd numbers and multiples of 3

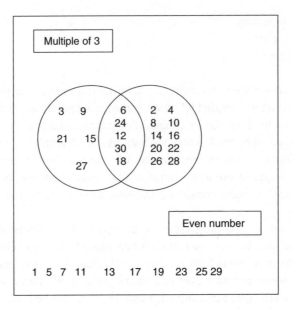

■ **Figure 8.3** Venn diagram used to sort odd numbers and multiples of 3

Reflective task

Translate the data shown in the bar chart in Figure 8.4 into a pie chart.

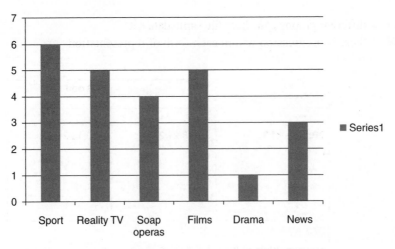

■ **Figure 8.4** Graph to show the number of 30-minute slots dedicated to each TV genre

Consider the progression in the representations of data listed above suggests that pie charts are more complex that bar charts. Is this idea challenged by this task?

Reflective task

List the four bar charts shown in Figure 8.5 in order of difficulty.

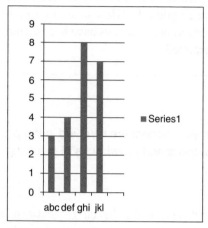

Graph 1

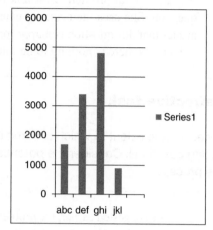

Graph 2

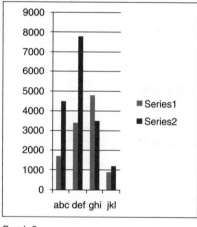

Graph 3

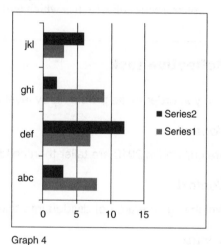

Graph 4

■ **Figure 8.5** Unlabelled bar charts

Where would you place each of these graphs in the suggested list of representations progression above?

The graphs have no titles/labels at this stage as we consider how the nature of the context might influence progression in the next section

Progression in contexts

As stated above, there may also be progression in the types of problems that children tackle. There is an interesting point to be made here about the extent to which children are involved in devising their own problems to solve. Surtees (2010) suggests that a potential problem with this is that the children may choose an inappropriate question. She uses the example where a child asks 'How many toys do I have?' and argues that this question is inappropriate as once the toys have been counted the cycle will end as there is nothing to be interpreted.

Reflective task

Reflect on the extent to which children in your school are involved in the process of posing questions. Consider the potential gains and drawbacks of involving them in this process.

As suggested earlier, the problem that is posed at the start of the data handling cycle is 'connected' to all the other stages of the cycle. In this next section we ask you to complete a series of activities which will deepen your understanding of these connections.

Reflective task

Can you order these problems by level of difficulty?

Context

Are children in 2010 are taller than children in 1837?

Context

Which flags are/are not divided into thirds?

Context

Winchester has 'better summers' than Newquay.

Context

How anxious is Red Riding Hood?

Context

Are these two pictures the same?

Context

There is too much sport on television.

As you undertake the activity it becomes apparent that, once again, this is not a straightforward task as the answer will depend on a range of factors including, for example, the nature of the two pictures, the kind of representation chosen, the level of analysis needed or the audience for the answer. This leads to the next section, which considers links between the nature of the problem posed and representation of the data in particular.

This reveals a number of anomalies. For example, the question 'How anxious is Red Riding Hood?' is a simple one and is in a context (a story book) that young children could understand. However, it could involve data that is measured over time and be presented as a line graph which indicated Red Riding Hood's level of anxiety over the course of the story. Similarly, the question about flags requires an understanding of unitary fractions but the representation of the data could be a single-criterion Carroll diagram.

Reflective task

Consider the contexts listed above. Complete Table 8.1 to indicate the kind of data that is collected and an appropriate form of representation.

■ **Table 8.1** Contexts for data handling

Context
How anxious is Red Riding Hood?

Data source:
Story book

Primary or secondary?
Categorical, discrete or continuous?

Representation
Sketch an appropriate representation

Context
Are my pictures the same?

Data source:
Birthday cards or wrapping paper

Primary or secondary?
Categorical, discrete or continuous?

Representation
Sketch an appropriate representation

Context
Are children in 2010 taller than children in 1837?

Data source:
1837 census

Primary or secondary?
Categorical, discrete or continuous?

Representation
Sketch an appropriate representation

Context
Which flags are/are not divided into thirds?

Data source:
Set of flags

Primary or secondary?
Categorical, discrete or continuous?

Representation
Sketch an appropriate representation

■ **Table 8.1** Cont'd

Context Winchester has 'better summers' than Newquay.	**Context** Crisps make a healthier breakfast than some cereals
Data source: Newspaper or website	**Data Source:** Nutritional information on cereal/crisp packets
Primary or secondary? Categorical, discrete or continuous?	Primary or secondary? Categorical, discrete or continuous?
Representation Sketch an appropriate representation	**Representation** Sketch an appropriate representation
Context Divide our class into teams of four for sports day. Each team must have at least one boy and one girl.	**Context** Noun verb or adjective?
Data Source: Primary – list of children	**Data source:** Primary – Set of words
Primary or secondary? Categorical, discrete or continuous?	Primary or secondary? Categorical, discrete or continuous?
Representation Sketch an appropriate representation	**Representation** Sketch an appropriate representation

Progression in interpretation of data

Early activities involving the interpretation of data are likely to involve the children in describing what they have found out by extracting the necessary information from a table, graph or chart. The next stage could require the children to extract a piece of information from the graph and then perform a calculation in order to answer the question posed. For example, the question might ask how many of an item are left for sale (rather than asking how many items were sold). If the data collected is numerical then it may be necessary to undertake some form of statistical analysis in order to provide an answer to the question posed. For example, if we wanted to explore the safety of travelling in a lift then a notion of mean weight would be needed, whereas if children wanted to identify the amount of each flavour of ice cream needed for the Year 6 barbecue then an understanding of mode would be needed. It could be argued that the next level of interpretation would involve the comparison of two sets of data and a search for a correlation. At some point in the interpretation of results, questions about the reliability of the data need to be discussed.

Again, an idea of progression in this single stage in the data handling cycle has been identified but once again the level of interpretation needed would depend on the question posed and the nature of the data. If we return to the set of contexts listed above then again it is clear that the level of interpretation required for each of the questions is different (indeed it could be argued that in some cases there is no interpretation required at all). This illustrates further both the 'connected' nature of the data handling cycle and the complexities of tracing learning trajectories.

As a specialist teacher you can take an overview of progression through the school and explore some of these complexities with teachers in your school. Your awareness of the points where the progression may not run smoothly and the connections between different aspects of the data handling cycling can help you to support your colleagues.

Using and applying mathematics

In Chapter 2 we defined the term using and applying mathematics as the part of the primary curriculum which relates to children's investigation and problem solving, or their work as mathematicians, thinking and reasoning mathematically. We also noted that the term would also refer to the process of teachers engaging with investigations and problems, undertaking mathematical enquiry which requires them to think mathematically. We put forward the argument that teachers and children need to engage in the process of solving non-routine problems which require mathematical thinking, generating general statements and constructing mathematical arguments in order to understand how these are constructed by mathematicians. Finally we suggested that mathematics is typified by enquiry.

The notion of enquiry is an interesting one to take forward in this chapter. Enquiry skills typically include an ability to ask relevant questions and to pose or define problems (Stage 1 in the data handling cycle); to plan what to do (Stage 2 of the data handling cycle); to research (Stage 3 of the data handling cycle); to identify conclusions (Stages 4 and 5 of the data handling cycle); to evaluate ideas (indicated in the cyclical nature of the data handling cycle). If we return to the opening part of this chapter, which considers key ideas in data handling, it could be argued that enquiry is the over-arching key feature of data handling.

It is also interesting to note links between the data handling cycle and what Polya (1957) describes as four principles for problem solving. These are listed as:

1   understand the problem
2   devise a plan
3   carry out the plan
4   review and extend.

Links between problem-solving processes and the data handling cycle are then very clear.

Orton and Frobisher (1999) suggest that problem solving involves reasoning processes such as analysis and reflection, and communication processes such as describing methods or identifying outcomes. These central themes of reasoning and reflection are echoed in curriculum documentation. In order to illustrate the reasoning and communication processes we will consider the context above, which stated that 'There is too much sport on TV.' If the class were organised into two teams and asked to argue the case for or against the statement, both 'teams' would be able to provide a reasoned argument based on available evidence to persuade the audience that they were 'right'. Deciding what data to collect in order to illustrate your point will provoke debate. There was a two-week period during 2010 when both Wimbledon and the World Cup were both taking place. Doubtless a great deal of sport will also be televised during the London Olympics. Making decisions such as when you will collect data will influence the outcome of the data collection event. This challenges the notion that some children may have about the nature of mathematics and highlights the importance of reasoning in constructing an understanding of mathematics.

Opportunities for communication are provided at each stage of the data handling cycle. For example, the teacher might start the session with a discussion about what constitutes sport and invite children to consider who they might ask or where they might look for a definition. Barmby *et al.* (2009) suggest that language development relating to handling data will emerge through this kind of discussion with children and note that the teacher has an important role in using the correct terminology throughout the process.

PEDAGOGICAL KNOWLEDGE

Knowledge of learners

This section will consider the suggestion put forward in Chapter 3, that pedagogical knowledge includes understanding of pupils' existing knowledge and their typical errors and misconceptions.

It would appear to be an oversimplification to suggest that in the case of data handling 'knowledge of learners' is simply about knowledge of children's prior experience of each of the stages of the data handling cycle. In this case 'knowledge of learners' would need to be extended to include an understanding of contexts and questions that are likely to be understood by and of interest to particular groups of children. So, for example, when considering a potential data handling task the teacher would need to know whether children understood the nature of the question posed as without this they would be unable to make decisions about the kind of data that they should collect. The teacher would need to know what kind of experiences children had of graphs and charts, as without this they would be unable to make decisions about the most appropriate way to represent the data. Skilful teaching will then allow children to bring their existing knowledge of both the context of the question and the knowledge of the processes involved in data handling to a new situation or 'mathematical world' (Sutherland 2007: 49) and develop new understanding.

There is potential for mistakes to be made in each of the five stages of the data handling session.

Reflective task

Add an example of potential mistakes at each stage of the data handling cycle to the list below

Posing the problem

Misunderstanding the context due to lack of experience.

Planning for data collection

Data collected does not address the question posed.

Gathering data

Inappropriate tallying of data. For example, when addressing the problem 'there is too much sport on TV' children may count each programme as one unit when the durations of the programmes are very different.

Representation of data

Representation of discrete data using a line graph.

Interpretation of data

Ignoring the scale on the y-axis or a key in a pictogram, e.g. treating every unit of representation as 1.

Surtees (2011) suggests that the use of inappropriate questions can lead to errors and misconceptions within the data handling cycle.

Reflective task

Reflect on the list of ten misconceptions that you have now listed. How many of them could be tracked back to some kind of misunderstanding of the question posed?

It would therefore seem sensible to suggest (Sutherland 2007) that carefully planned discussion of the question is needed at the outset of any data handling task. As a specialist teacher you will have an important role in supporting teachers to devise appropriate contexts for exploring aspects of the data handling cycle.

Models, images and analogies used to teach aspects of data handling

In Chapter 3 we established the need for teachers to make use of a range of resources, representations and analogies alongside appropriate explanations and questions in order to transform personal deep subject knowledge into a form that is accessible to learners.

In order to exemplify this we will focus on a set of scenarios that could be used to explore mean. For each image, analogy or question listed below the key idea about 'mean' that it could suggest is also noted.

Scenario 1: Pocket money club

Peter (who does not receive any pocket money) starts a 'pocket money' club at his school. In order to be a member of the club you need to give your pocket money to Peter, who then divides the money out between the group.

Key ideas:

■ Sharing the full set of data out equally.
■ In a set of data with a mean of x some data will be greater than x and some will be less.

Scenario 2: Visitors for the head teacher

Three visitors with a mean age of 30 are waiting to see the head teacher. What could their ages be?

■ They could be all the same (three people all aged thirty).
■ They could be nearly the same (three people aged 28, 29 and 33).
■ They could be very different (a baby aged 1, a mum aged 27 and granny aged 62).
■ Two could be close and one far away (two adults aged 40 and a child of 10).

Key idea:

■ Lots of different data sets can have the same mean.

Scenario 3: Shoe sizes

The owner of a shoe shop is ordering sandals for sale in the summer. He is looking at last year's figures for sales of each size. Which measure of average will be of most use to him?

Key idea:

■ Different measures of average are needed in different contexts.

The message here is that it is often necessary to make use of a range of images, questions, etc. so that children develop a full understanding of an area of mathematics and reduce the potential for invalid generalisations to arise.

Effective task design

In Chapter 3 we suggested that tasks should elicit activity from the learner and noted what 'activity' might look like. We also suggested that effective tasks should draw learners' attention to important features, so that they may learn to distinguish between relevant aspects, or recognise properties or appreciate relationships between properties. Finally, we identified the need for teachers to devise sequences of tasks so that over time, students' experiences 'add up to something important'. The next section will consider what makes an effective data handling task.

Again, in general research which refers to problem solving, can be applied to the data handling cycle in particular. Orton and Frobisher (1999) note that an investigation is characterised by a 'spirit of dynamic engagement on the part of the investigator'. They go on to suggest there is also a strong element of curiosity evoked as the investigation moves into the unknown and there are a range of paths to choose to follow. It seems sensible to suggest that the same can be said of a data handling task and so the notion of 'activity' on the part of the learner can be extended to include 'curiosity'.

Evidence put forward so far in this chapter would suggest that:

■   effective tasks will have the scope for children to actively engage with all stages of the data handling cycle or to focus on particular aspects of the data handling cycle;

■   the designing of questions to pose to children is a particularly important part of the process of effective task design;

■   effective tasks promote decision making, reasoning and communication as 'activities' on the part of the learner.

Reflective task

Reflect on the first point listed above. Consider whether effective data handling tasks should have the scope to engage children with all aspects of the data handling cycle. Or could an effective data handling task focus on one or two particular features of the data handling cycle? How is a balance between the two achieved in your school?

This may be an interesting avenue for you to pursue in your school in terms of the need for teachers to devise sequences of tasks. It would seem to be an oversimplification to suggest that all sequences should pursue the same five stages of enquiry in the same order when in fact a sequence of tasks which focused on one element in particular could lead to a depth of understanding of that particular key idea. For example, a sequence of tasks which required children to plan data collection sheets could be very useful. Using the example above, children could spend some time considering what changes they would make in the data collection process if the question was changed from 'There is too much sport on TV' to 'There is more sport on TV than anything else.' Time could be spent very productively in debating the nature of the evidence needed to build a case for and against each argument, perhaps without actually going on to gather and present the information. It could be argued that this kind of task would leave behind 'important residue' (Hiebert *et al.* 1997: 31) which would then be used in subsequent tasks which required children to engage with all five aspects of the data handling cycle.

In Chapter 3 we considered the question of whether mathematical tasks should be placed in contexts or whether the context could become a distraction from the mathematical content. Cotton (2010: 90) argues that data handling is possibly the only area of mathematics that can be taught through a totally cross-curricular approach. One obvious example of links with another subject would be the 'persuasive writing' or 'speaking and listening' strands of the English curriculum. A study of use of data in the media would reveal that data is often used (alongside written or spoken English) to persuade the reader of a particular point of view (for example, that Supermarket A is somehow 'better' than Supermarket B). He goes on to put forward the suggestion that data handling may only be taught in this way. Indeed it does seem sensible to suggest that it cannot be taught without a context (or a problem to solve).

Reflective task

Consider your own position in this debate. Is data handling the *only* aspect of the mathematics curriculum that can be taught in a totally cross-curricular way? Can data handling *only* be taught in a cross-curricular way or are there some skills that have to be taught discretely?

These questions are interesting ones as it could be argued that data handling or 'statistics' are somehow different from other aspects of mathematics as they do not have any 'life' outside of the context; i.e 'data handling' is a set of tools for the task of answering contextualised questions, whereas number, for example, can generate activity from children in its own right. The following sequences of consecutive numbers 23, 24, 25 and 47, 48, 49 are interesting as they both follow the same pattern 'prime, lots of factors, square' and children could pursue this line of enquiry; however, the fact that 1, 33, 65 and 32, 33, 34 have the same mean is possibly not very interesting until it has a context.

COACHING AND MENTORING SCENARIOS

Use the arguments considered in this chapter to think about how you might support and challenge colleagues in these scenarios. What sort of good practice would you want to share from your own classroom? What arguments might you put forward? What literature could you call on? Would written guidance help to support them? Which mentoring or coaching strategies might be most appropriate?

Scenario 1

In John's school, the head teacher has created a strong team-learning culture. John, a very experienced Year 2 teacher, has been paired with you for a collaborative project to enhance teaching and learning in an aspect of mathematics of your choice. You have agreed a goal of 'developing more effective tasks for data handling in KS1'. What might your next steps be?

Scenario 2

Melanie has wanted to be a teacher for as long as she can remember. She is in her first year of teaching. Melanie has just had her first half-termly meeting with her head teacher about pupil progress. It appears that some children in the class are not making satisfactory progress in MA4. She has come to you in your role as mentor for Newly Qualified Teachers. What might the next steps be?

Scenario 3

Whole-school analysis of children's performance in KS2 National Curriculum tests and work scrutiny in school suggests that, while children do carry out data collection tasks and present information in various ways, evidence of children's ability to interpret data is limited. In your role as MaST or subject leader or subject manager you have been asked to take this forward at a whole-school level. What might your next steps be?

CONCLUSIONS

A strong theme that runs through this chapter is the 'connected' nature of the five stages of the data handling cycle. We considered the impact that this has in identifying progression in data handling. Links between the data handling cycle and models of problem solving have also been explored. We have identified a range of potential misconceptions in data handling and suggested that many of these can be traced back to a lack of shared understanding between the teacher and the child about the nature of the question posed. We suggest that there is a need for thoughtfully chosen questions for children to consider and that discussion and debate are key to both identifying misconceptions and moving learning forward.

FURTHER READING

Surtees, L. (2011) 'Handling data', in A. Hansen (ed.) *Children's Errors in Mathematics.* Exeter: Learning Matters. This chapter explores potential errors and misconceptions in data handling in more detail.

Price, R. and Raiker, A. (2003) 'Is teacher confidence a factor in the effective teaching of data handling?', *Topic* 29: 7–11. This considers the teacher subject knowledge and confidence in data handling in particular.

An internet search for 'Polya' will allow you to explore the work of this celebrated author in further depth and to compare this with other modules of problem solving and the stages in the data handling cycle listed in this chapter.Reflective task

Consider your own confidence in teaching aspects of data handling. Reflect on the amount and nature of any training you may have had or delivered in data handling. Did data handling form a significant part of your Initial Teacher Training? What about subsequent CPD?

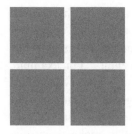

CONCLUSION

The aim of this chapter is to provide a framework for you to reflect on your perspectives on the teaching and learning of primary mathematics and your role as a specialist teacher. This chapter will draw together the key themes raised in previous chapters and provide an opportunity for you to:

- consider the values and principles that underpin your 'vision' of the teaching and learning of primary mathematics;
- identify ways in which ideals can be sustained and developed;
- consider the role of the subject specialist in championing the cause of mathematics in whole-school settings and in the wider local context.

The words 'sustained' and 'developed' are both important here as the 'vision' for primary mathematics that we will ask you to consider will need to be reviewed as it is challenged by new personal experiences and other research evidence. In this way values and principles are seen as 'dynamic' as they evolve over time, are politically and socially influenced and subject to change as a result of professional judgements made. We will consider this self-evaluation process in two phases:

- curriculum content
- approaches to learning and teaching.

The dynamic nature of primary mathematics can be exemplified through an exploration of various models of the primary mathematics curriculum over time. Indeed, Shuard (1986: 29) begins her description of the primary mathematics curriculum by acknowledging its fluctuating nature, 'it is clear [...] that the primary mathematics curriculum for the 1990s will need to be different both in emphasis and content from that of the early 1980s'. Brown described these changes as 'swings of the pendulum' in 1999, and then revised this expression to 'swings and roundabouts' in 2010. She also notes the political influences whereby government through the various agencies in England exercise a degree of influence on both the content of the curriculum and teachers' actions. Certainly this can be illustrated through reference to various government publications over the last half century. For example, Floyd states that 'Curriculum Bulletin No.1 (1965) gave rise to discovery learning' with its suggestion that 'Although discovery methods take longer in the initial stages (between the ages of 5 and 8 or 9) far less practice is required to obtain and maintain efficiency in computation when children have been enabled to make their own discoveries' (1981: 10). In 1967 the Plowden report advocated a 'child centred education', which included an emphasis on pupil autonomy; children were expected to work independently or in small groups, with the teacher being seen as a resource to call upon when stuck (CACE 1967).

Next came the Cockcroft report (1982) and a 'swing in the pendulum' towards problem solving, which was described as 'at the heart of mathematics' (p. 249). This signified a new utilitarian emphasis as 'mathematics is only "useful" to the extent to which it can be applied to a particular situation and it is the ability to apply mathematics to a variety of situations to which we give the name "problem solving"' (para. 249). With the White Paper *Better Schools* (DES 1985) came the first announcement of the intention to formulate both national objectives to be known as 'attainment targets' and an associated system of assessment. This was followed by various versions of the National Curriculum between 1989 and 2000 and the introduction of national testing in 1991. The pendulum began to swing again in 1996 when concerns were raised about low standards of numeracy and about teaching methods. The NNS Framework for Teaching Mathematics (DfEE 1999) described not only a detailed year-by-year curriculum but also advocated 'direct teaching' which included 'directing and instructing' (p. 11). These approaches to teaching and learning were an almost complete reversal of the roles described in the Plowden report. At the beginning of the next century came a series of documents under the title *Excellence and Enjoyment* (DfES 2003) which stated 'our goal is for every primary school to combine excellence in teaching with enjoyment in learning' and a central message was that 'teachers have the power to decide how they teach' (p. 16). In 2006 it was decided that further change was needed with greater cohesion across the curriculum. The Primary National Strategy (DfES 2006) documentation was a joint venture between mathematics and English. The provision of training and materials was far lower key than in 1999 and there is only limited evidence of any change in practice. For mathematics the publication of the Williams Review in 2008 was significant as its recommendations sought to strengthen teacher subject knowledge and gave rise to the mathematics specialist teacher and an emphasis on teacher subject knowledge and pedagogy. It appeared that the pendulum was due to swing again following recommendations from Alexander and Rose in 2009 for a more progressive and less prescriptive curriculum with greater emphasis on conceptual development and the process of learning. However, a change of government has left these ideas somewhat 'in the air' as a new phase of evidence gathering and expert consultation is embarked upon.

Brown (2010: 3) argues that the tensions about curriculum content can be summarised by two positions which can be broadly characterised as 'procedural' where an emphasis is placed on the accurate use of methods of calculation and 'conceptual' which stresses the importance of an understanding of the underlying mathematical content. She goes on to suggest that tensions about how children are taught can again be grouped into two broad categories. First there are the 'progressive' philosophies which emphasise the importance of autonomy both of pupils and teachers, and second there are 'public education' philosophies which emphasise the need for a greater degree of state intervention in the curriculum and in teaching methods in order to both protect the equal entitlement of pupils and to 'meet the skilled person power requirements of the state' (2010: 3).

Reflective task

Consider the dichotomies listed above as continuums. Where would you place your priorities on the two number lines below?

Procedural   Conceptual
_____

Progressive   Public education
_____

The Cockcroft report draws attention to the fact that effective mathematics teaching needs to attend to a number of different elements of mathematics which are listed as: 'facts; skills; conceptual structures; general strategies for problem solving and investigation; appreciation of the nature of mathematics; and attitudes towards mathematics' (1982 paras 240–1). Shuard bemoans the fact that very often when a particular mathematics curriculum is described 'it is very common for only the first three of these elements – facts, skills and conceptual structures – to be listed. These elements form the content of primary mathematics' (1986: 29). She goes on to liken problem-solving skills to the 'processes involved in doing mathematics' and suggests that these should also be given suitable emphasis in any primary mathematics curriculum design. She also introduces two further dimensions to the primary mathematics curriculum. The first is what she calls 'situations': 'for children mathematics is set in the context of a variety of situations and experiences, and is built upon these situations and experiences' (p. 29) and the second is 'appreciation and attitudes' which she suggests should 'permeate all the mathematics that is done in school' (p. 30). Orton and Frobisher lend their support to this argument when they suggest that 'like all subjects such as art and music, mathematics can be appreciated and enjoyed for its own sake (1996: 5). These quotations from Shuard and Orton and Frobisher provide some insight into their personal values.

Having explored a range of possible perspectives on the teaching and learning of mathematics the next task is designed to allow you to begin to consider your 'vision' of a primary mathematics curriculum for your school.

Reflective task

Consider this as a series of questions.

What is the purpose of primary mathematics education?

Why does mathematics justify a place in the primary curriculum?

List some important learning outcomes for primary-aged children.

Use the answers to the questions listed above to articulate your vision of a curriculum for mathematics in your school.

In your role as primary mathematics specialist it will also be important for you to share and develop a vision of mathematics teaching and learning for your school. Evidence (Showers *et al.* 1987) suggests that shared understandings do facilitate teachers' willingness to try out new ideas. These ideas of individual and collective 'vision' are echoed by Hunzicher (2010), who argues that effective professional development should be supportive of both individual needs and concerns alongside those of the school.

The next stage in the self-evaluation process is to make judgements on the nature of learning experiences in your class and your school. We begin with an exploration of learning from a theoretical perspective which builds on the idea that children are involved in the process of developing new knowledge and understanding knowledge introduced in Chapter 2.

Jaworski (1994) cites Von Glasersfeld (1987), who suggests that 'knowledge is not passively received but actively built up by the cognising subject' (p. 14). This implies that we all construct our own knowledge. We do not passively receive it from our environment. A further implication is that learners' new understandings are dependent on prior knowledge and experiences. What we each *know* is the accumulation of all our experiences so far. Every new encounter either adds to that experience or challenges it. Supposing a child wants to find, for example, the total of 564 and 342, he or she might use a number of methods which have been part of previous experience. This experience might suggest that there is only one answer to the question, but if the various methods when applied throw up more that one value then here experience is challenged. He or she then has to re-examine the methods used and current understanding of total. If as a result a method is discarded because it is now thought to be inappropriate then his or her experience has been modified. The child will have come to learn more about finding the total. Next time he or she comes to a question about finding the total it will be with this new experience, which will condition his or her thinking.

In a social environment (such as a classroom) learners are challenged by other individuals. Through the use of language and social interchange new knowledge is constructed and the viability of knowledge is tested. This negotiation of shared meaning within a social context often provides a source of cognitive dissonance that allows individual students to restructure their conceptual structures and so reach higher levels of understanding.

It could be argued (Jaworski 1994; Von Glasersfeld 1987) that adopting a constructivist perspective has important consequences for teachers:

- The teacher will realise that knowledge cannot be transferred to the student by a 'transmission' approach as this does not provide any interaction between prior and new knowledge.
- The teacher will use language as a tool in the process of guiding the student's construction.
- The teacher will try to maintain the view that students are attempting to make sense in their experiential world. Hence he or she will be interested in the mistakes that children make because these provide insight into how the children, at the point in their development, are organising their experiential world.

Having considered one philosophical perspective on learning, the next task is to consider the nature of learning experiences in your school. This is achieved by reflecting on a series of questions.

Reflective task

For each question a straightforward answer of yes or no is unlikely. Instead the answer is likely to consider particular teachers, specific groups of pupils and different aspects of the mathematics curriculum.

Attitudes

Do pupils have positive attitudes about mathematics?

Do pupils have high expectations of themselves and what they can achieve?

Do pupils engage in mathematical tasks with interest and enthusiasm?

Subject knowledge

Do pupils make good progress?

Do pupils make connections between different aspects of mathematics?

Are pupils able to use and apply their mathematical skills across the curriculum?

Pedagogy

Do pupils make choices about which tools to use to support their learning?

Are mathematical tasks made meaningful and relevant to children?

Do learning environments celebrate success, inspire further interest and support learning?

Are pupils learning needs identified and addressed?

Your answers to the questions listed should enable you to consider what you and your school do well and identify any areas for development.

The next section will consider how teachers or schools can maintain a vision for mathematics teaching and learning in the face of initiatives that can appear conflicting or prescriptive, a taught curriculum that may appear to be defined by summative assessment and apparently intimidating inspection procedures.

The NCETM (2011) put forward a long list of what they describe as unhelpful principles that have somehow become almost a set of classroom 'rules'. We suggest that in some cases it might be the case that this may be the result of a misinterpretation of the initiative or idea (rather than an overly prescriptive regime). For example, the NCETM (2011) suggest that one commonly held belief is that 'you must start your lesson by sharing the learning intention'. Analysis of original research on the importance of shared learning goals would not support this rather narrow interpretation. NCETM (2011) also put forward the idea that many teachers believe (especially in the period 1999–2006) that a lesson must have exactly three parts. Again, rigorous analysis of the documentation available at this time would reveal a far more cautious approach. Ofsted (2001) claim that more successful schools undertake in-school tasks which invite teachers to reflect upon initiatives and adapt them to meet their particular school needs.

Reflective task

Exploring the factors that challenge personal and whole-school values

NCETM (2011) report that simplistic interpretations of government documentation and the perceived inflexibility and mechanistic nature of inspection regimes (including internal procedures) can inhibit principled and imaginative teaching.

Reflect on the extent to which this is the case in your school.

Consider the extent to which new initiatives, curriculum documentation and procedures for performance review are jointly explored and agreed by staff.

Participants in the NCETM (2011) research suggested a range of potential ways forward which included:

■　All those in mathematics education should continue to seek ways of promoting positive images of mathematics and mathematicians to society in general.

■　Effective collaborative professional development should focus both on developing participants' subject and pedagogical knowledge, rather than the mechanics of implementing the latest 'initiative' learning.

■　There is a need for the teaching profession to share experiences and effective resources for learning.

Reflective task

Making progress

Take the three ideas in turn and note what you have already done and what else you might do. Draw on the ideas raised in Chapter 5.

	What I have done	What else I could do
Promote positive images of mathematics and mathematicians		
Collaborative professional development		
Sharing experiences and effective resources for learning		

CONCLUSION

This chapter has considered the ideas of subject knowledge and pedagogy through reference to curriculum documentation and an exploration of learning from a theoretical perspective. We have taken you through a series of tasks which were designed to allow you to reflect on your personal principles and values. We have suggested that it is important for a school to devise a shared set of core values and that these need to be reviewed on a regular basis. As a subject specialist it is important that your practice exemplifies those principles and values and that, much in the way that you would tackle misconceptions in your own classroom, you will also need to challenge any unhelpful 'myths' that might become embedded in practice over time. The longer-term vision is that as a mathematics specialist you work alongside other skilled teachers to champion the cause of mathematics in a wider local context, and that these local hubs of influence lead to improvements nationally with positive attitudes, high expectations and world-class mathematics education and high standards for all.

FURTHER READING

Brown, M. (2010) 'Swings and roundabouts', in I. Thompson (ed.) *Issues in Teaching Numeracy*. Buckingham: OUP. This chapter gives a detailed account of the changes in curriculum priorities over time from the perspective of the author.

NCETM (2011) *Mathematics Matters: Final Report*. This document includes an account of the tasks undertaken by the research group in order to develop a set of values and principles. The tasks could be adapted and used in your own school.

BIBLIOGRAPHY

ACME (2005) *Ensuring a High Quality, Localised Infrastructure for the Continuing Profes-sional Development of Teachers of Mathematics.* Available at http://www.acme-uk.org/media/1457/ensuring%20high%20quality,%20localised%20infrastructure%20for%20the%20cpd%20of%20teachers%20of%20mathematics.pdf (accessed 26 July 2011).

ACME (2008) *Mathematics in Primary Years.* London: ACME.

Ainley, J. and Luntley, M. (2005) *What Teachers Know: The Knowledge Bases of Classroom Practice in Proceedings of CERME-4.* Saint Felieu de Gixols, Spain.

Albone, S. and Tymms, P. (2004) *The Impact of the National Numeracy Strategy on Children's Attitudes to Mathematics.* Manchester: British Educational Research Association Annual Conference

Alexander, R. (2009) *Children, Their World, Their Education: Final Report and Recommen-dations of the Cambridge Primary Review.* London: Routledge.

Allison, S. and Harbour, M. (2009) *The Coaching Toolkit.* London: Sage.

Anghileri, J. (2000) *Teaching Number Sense.* London: Continuum.

Ashcroft, M. and Moore, A. (2009) 'Mathematics anxiety and the affective drop in performance', *Journal of Psychoeducational Assessment* 27(3): 197–205.

Askew, M., Brown, M., Johnson, D., Rhodes, V. and Wiliam, D. (1997) *Effective Teachers of Numeracy Final Report.* London: Kings College.

Askew, M. and Wiliam, D. (1995) 'Learning is more effective when common misconceptions are address, exposed and discussed in teaching', *Qwest* 4: 14–19.

Aubrey, C. (1997) *Mathematics Teaching in the Early Years: An Investigation of Teachers' Subject Knowledge.* London: Falmer Press.

Ball, D.L., Hill, H.C. and Bass, H. (2005) 'Who knows mathematics well enough to teach third grade, and how can we decide?' *American Educator.* Available online at: http://aft.org/pubs-reports/american_educator/issues/fall2005/BallF05.pdf (accessed 23 March 2010).

Ball, D., Hoover Thames, M. and Phelps, G. (2008) 'Content knowledge for teaching: what makes it special?', *Journal of Teacher Education* 59: 389–407.

Barmby, P., Bilsborugh, L., Harries, T. and Higgins, S. (2009) *Primary Mathematics Teaching for Understanding.* Maidenhead: OUP.

Barmby, P., Bilsborugh, L., Harries, T. and Higgins, S. (2010) 'Teaching for understanding/understanding for teaching', in I. Thompson (ed.) *Issues in Teaching Numeracy in Primary Schools.* Maidenhead: OUP.

Biggs, E. and Sutton, J. (1983) *Teaching Mathematics 5 to 9.* London: McGraw-Hill.

Bottle, G. (2005) *Teaching Mathematics in the Primary School*. London: Continuum.

Brown, M. (1999) 'Swings of the pendulum', in I. Thompson (ed.) *Issues in Teaching Numeracy*. Buckingham: OUP.

Brown, M. (2010) 'Swings and roundabouts', in I. Thompson (ed.) *Issues in Teaching Numeracy*. 2nd edn. Buckingham: OUP.

Bruner, J. (1974) 'Representation in childhood', in *Beyond the Information Given*. London: George Allen and Unwin.

Bruner, J. (1996) *The Culture of Education*. London: Harvard University Press.

Brockbank, A. and McGill, I. (2006) *Facilitating Reflective Learning through Mentoring and Coaching*. London: Kogan Page.

Bubb, S. and Earley, P. (2010) *Helping Staff Develop in Schools*. London: Sage.

Burley, S. and Pomphrey, C. (2011) *Mentoring and Coaching in Schools: Professional Learning through Collaborative Enquiry*. London: Routledge.

Buxton, L. (1981) *Do You Panic about Maths? Coping with Maths Anxiety*. London: Heinemann Education.

Buxton, L. (1985) *Cognitive-affective Interaction in Foundations of Human Learning*. Unpublished doctoral thesis: Warwick University.

CACE (1967) *Children and their Primary Schools* (Plowden report). London: HMSO.

Carpenter, T.P. and Moser, J.M. (1983) 'The acquisition of addition and subtraction concepts', in R. Lesh and M. Landau (eds) *Acquisition of Mathematical Concepts and Processes*. New York: Academic Press.

Clarke, S. (2001) *Unlocking Formative Assessment*. London: Hodder & Stoughton.

Cockburn, A. (1999) *Teaching Mathematics with Insight*. London: Falmer Press.

Cockcroft, W.H. (1982) *Mathematics Counts, Report of the Committee of Inquiry into the Teaching of Mathematics under the Chairmanship of Dr. W. H. Cockroft*. London: HMSO.

Cotton, T. (2010) *Understanding and Teaching Primary Mathematics*. Essex: Pearson Education Limited.

Cox, E., Bachirova, T. and Clutterbuck, D. (eds) (2010) *The Complete Handbook of Coaching*. London: Sage.

Daily Telegraph (2008) *Poor Maths Standards Threaten UK Economy*. 5 June.

Davis, B. and Simmt, E. (2006) 'Mathematics-for-teaching: an ongoing investigation of the mathematics that teachers (need to) know', *Educational Studies in Mathematics* 61(3): 293–319.

Davis, R.B. (1992) 'Understanding "understanding"', *Journal of Mathematical Behaviour* 11: 225–241.

Desforges, C. (2003) *The Impact of Parental Involvement, Parental Support and Family Education on Pupil Achievements and Adjustment*. London: DfES.

DCSF (2007) *The National Strategies: Using a Lesson Study CPD Approach in Mathematics with a Focus on Number*. Available at http://nso.archive.teachfind.com/node/102702 (accessed 1 September 2011).

DCSF (2008) *Primary National Strategy: Primary Framework for Literacy and Mathematics*. Available at http://nso.archive.teachfind.com/primary/primaryframework (accessed 1 September 2011).

DCSF (2009) *Numbers and Patterns: Laying Foundations in Mathematics*. Nottingham: DCSF Publications.

DCSF (2010) *The Mathematics Specialist Teacher Programme Internal Information for Providers*. London: DCSF Publications.

DES (1982) *Mathematics Counts (Cockcroft report)*. London: HMSO.

DES (1985) *Better Schools*. London: HMSO.

DfE (2010) *The Importance of Teaching: The Schools White Paper*. London: HMSO.

DfEE (1999) *National Numeracy Strategy Framework for Teaching Mathematics*. London: DfEE.

DfES (2003) *Excellence and Enjoyment: A Strategy for Primary Schools*. Nottingham: DfES.

DfES (2004) *Choosing Examples*. London: DfES.

DfES (2005) *National Framework for Mentoring and Coaching*. Available at http://www. curee-paccts.com/resources/publications/national-framework-mentoring-and-coaching (accessed 1 September 2011).

DfES (2006) *Primary National Strategy: Primary Framework of Literacy and Mathematics*. London: DfES.

Donaldson, G. (2002) *Successful Mathematics Leadership in Primary Schools*. Exeter: Learning Matters.

Drew, D. and Hansen, A. (2007) *Using Resources to Support Mathematical Thinking Primary and Early Years*. Exeter: Learning Matters.

Drews, D. (2005) 'Errors and misconceptions, the teacher's role', in A. Hansen (ed.) *Children's Errors in Mathematics*. Exeter: Learning Matters.

Duncan, A. (1996) *What Primary Teachers Should Know About Maths*. 2nd edn. London: Hodder and Stoughton.

Early Years Curriculum Group (1993) *Early Education in Jeopardy: An Action Paper for Early Years Practitioners, Action Paper Number 1*.

Elton, B. (2009) *Meltdown*. London: Bantam Press.

Floyd, A. (ed.) (1981) *Developing Mathematical Thinking*. Wokingham: Oxford University Press.

Fox, S. and Surtees, S. (2010) *Mathematics across the Curriculum*. New York: Continuum.

Fraser, H. and Honeyford, G. (2000) *Children, Parents and Teachers Enjoying Numeracy*. London: David Fulton Publishers Ltd.

Freudenthal, H. (1991) *Revisiting Mathematics Education: China Lectures*. Dordrecht: Kluwer Academic Publishers.

Garvey, R. (2010) 'Mentoring in a coaching world', in E. Cox, T. Bachirova and D. Clutterbuck (eds) *The Complete Handbook of Coaching*. London: Sage, pp. 341–354.

Gelman, R. and Gallistel C. (1978) *The Children's Understanding of Number*. Cambridge, MA. and London: Harvard University Press.

Gifford, S. (2005) *Teaching Mathematics 3–5 Developing Learning in the Foundation Stage*. Maidenhead: Open University Press.

Gray, E. and Tall, D. (2007) 'Abstraction as a natural process of mental compression', *Mathematics Education Research Journal* 19(2): 23–40.

GTC (2010) *Professionalism and Pedagogy: A commentary by the Teaching and Learning Research Programme and the General Teaching Council for England*. London: IOE.

Guardian (1999) *Teachers Too Ashamed to Admit Inability in Maths*. 2 September.

Guardian (2008) *Every Primary School to Have a Specialist Maths Teacher, The Way Forward*. 17 June.

Hannula, M.S. (2002) 'Attitudes towards mathematics: emotions, expectations and values', *Educational Studies in Mathematics* 49: 25–46.

Hansen, A. (ed.) (2011) *Children's Errors in Mathematics*. Exeter: Learning Matters.

Haylock, D. (2010) *Mathematics Explained for Primary Teachers*. 4th edn. London: Sage Publications.

Haylock, D. and Cockburn, A. (2008) *Understanding Mathematics for Young Children: A Guide for Foundation Stage and Lower Primary Teachers*. London: Sage.

Headington, R. (2001) *Supporting Numeracy: A Handbook for Those who Assist in Early Years Settings*. 2nd edn. London: David Fulton Publishers Ltd.

Hiebert, J. (1997) *Making Sense: Teaching and Learning Mathematics with Understanding*. Portsmouth, NH: Heinemann.

Hiebert, J., Carpenter, T., Fennema, E., Fuson, K., Wearne, D., Murray, H., Olivieir, A. and Human, P. (1997) *Making Meaning: Teaching and Learning Mathematics with Understanding*. Portsmouth, NH: Heineman.

Hodgen, J. and Wiliam, D. (2006) *Mathematics Inside the Black Box: Assessment for Learning in the Mathematics Classroom.* London: NFER Nelson.

Houssart, J. (2007) 'They don't use their brains what a pity: school mathematics through the eyes of the older generation', *Research in Mathematics Education* 9: 47–63.

Hunzicker, J. (2011) 'Effective professional development for teachers: a checklist', *Professional Development in Education* 37(2): 171–177

Jaworski, B. (1994) *Investigating Mathematics Teaching: A Constructivist Enquiry.* London: Falmer Press.

Karp, K., Allen, C., Allen, L. and Brown, E.T. (1998) 'Feisty females: inspiring girls to think mathematically', *Teaching Children Mathematics* 11(3): 118–126.

Katz, L.G. (1995) *Talks with Teachers of Young Children.* Norwood, NJ: Albex Publishing Corporation.

Kerry, T. and Shelton Mayes, A. (eds) (1995) *Issues in Mentoring.* London: Routledge.

Koshy, V. (1999) *Effective Teaching of Numeracy.* London: Hodder & Stoughton.

Koshy, V., Ernest, P. and Casey, R. (2000) *Mathematics for Primary Teachers.* London: Routledge.

Koshy, V. and Murray, J. (2002) *Unlocking Numeracy.* London: Fulton.

Lee, C. (2006) *Language for Learning Mathematics: Assessment for Learning in Practice.* Maidenhead: Open University Press.

Lewis, A. (1996) *Discovering Mathematics with 4 to 7 year olds.* London: Hodder & Stoughton.

Lim, C. (2002) 'Public images of mathematics', *Philosophy of Mathematics Education Journal.* Available at http://www.people.ex.ac.uk/PErnest/pome15/public_images.htm (accessed July 2011).

Lim, C.S. and Ernest, P. (2000) 'A survey of public images of mathematics', *Education Papers of The British Society for Research into Learning Mathematics* 2: 193–206.

Ma, L. (1999*) Knowing and Teaching Elementary Mathematics: Teachers' Understanding of Fundamental Mathematics in China and the United States.* Mahwah, NJ: Lawrence Erlbaum Associates.

Mason, J. and Johnston-Wilder, S. (2006) *Designing and Using Mathematical Tasks.* Hatfield: Tarquin.

Maxwell, K. (2001) 'Positive learning dispositions in mathematics', *ACE Papers* 11: 30–39.

Nardi, E. and Steward, S. (2003) 'Is mathematics T.I.R.E.D.? A profile of quiet disaffection in the secondary mathematics classroom', *British Educational Research Journal* 29: 345–367.

NCETM (2010a) 'Anglo-Saxon attitudes?' Available online at https://www.ncetm.org.uk/resources/24990 (accessed 22 July 2011).

NCETM (2010b) 'Equal opportunities'. Available online at https://www.ncetm.org.uk/resources/24991 (accessed 22 July 2011).

NCETM (2010c) 'Maths4Us launched to improve adult numeracy'. Available online at https://www.ncetm.org.uk/news/26531 (accessed 21 December 2011).

NCETM (2011) 'Mathematics Matters: Final Report'. Available online at: https://www.ncetm.org.uk/public/files/309231/Mathematics+Matters+Final+Report.pdf

Nunes, T. and Bryant, P. (1996) *Children Doing Mathematics.* Oxford: Blackwell Publishers.

Nunes, T., Bryant, P. and Watson, A. (2009) *Key Understandings in Mathematics.* London: Nuffield Foundation.

Ofsted (1997) *The Teaching of Number in Three Inner-Urban LEAs.* London: OFSTED.

Ofsted (2001) *National Numeracy Strategy: The Second Year.* London: OFSTED.

Ofsted (2008) *Mathematics: Understanding the Score.* London: OFSTED.

Ofsted (2010a) *Finnish Pupils' Success in Mathematics.* Manchester: OFSTED.

Ofsted (2010b) *Good Professional Development in Schools: How Does Leadership Contribute?* London: OFSTED.

Orton, A. and Frobisher, L. (1996) *Insights into Teaching Mathematics.* London: Cassell.

Pask, R. and Joy, B. (2007) *Mentoring-Coaching: A Guide for Education Professionals.* Maidenhead: Open University Press.

Pollard, A. (2008) *Reflective Teaching.* London: Continuum.

Polya, G. (1957) *How to Solve It.* New York: Doubleday Anchor Books.

Poulson, L. (2001) 'Paradigm lost? Subject knowledge, primary teachers and education policy', *British Journal of Educational Studies* 49(1): 45–55.

Pound, L. (2008) *Thinking and Learning about Mathematics in the Early Years.* London: Routledge

Price, R. and Raiker, A. (2003) 'Is teacher confidence a factor in the effective teaching of data handling?', *Topic* 29: 7–11.

Richards, P. (1982) 'Difficulties in learning mathematics', in M. Cornelius (ed.) *Teaching Mathematics.* London and Canberra: Croom Helm, pp. 59–80.

Rose, J. (2009) *The Rose Report on the Primary School Curriculum.* London: DCSF.

Rowland, T., Turner, F., Thwaites, A. and Huckstep, P. (2009) *Developing Primary Mathematics Teaching.* London: Sage.

Royal Society (2010) *Primary Science and Mathematics Education: Getting the Basics Right.* London: The Royal Society.

Shaw, R. (1995) 'Mentoring', in T. Kerry and A. Shelton Mayes (eds) *Issues in Mentoring.* London: Routledge, pp. 259–267.

Showers, B., Joyce, B. and Bennett B. (1987) 'Synthesis of research on staff development: a framework for future study and a state-of-the-art analysis', *Educational Leadership* November: 77–87.

Shuard, H. (1986) *Primary Mathematics Today and Tomorrow.* Harlow: Longman.

Shulman, L. (1986) 'Those who understand: knowledge growth in teaching', *Educational Researcher* 15: 4–14.

Shulman, L. (1987) 'Knowledge and teaching: foundations of the new reform', *Harvard Educational Review* 57(1): 1–22.

Skemp, R. (1989) *Mathematics in the Primary School.* London: Routledge.

Suggate, J., Davis, A. and Goulding, M. (2010) *Mathematical Knowledge for Primary Teachers.* 4th edn. London: Routledge.

Surtees, L. (2011) 'Handling data', in A. Hansen (ed.) *Children's Errors in Mathematics.* Exeter: Learning Matters.

Sutherland, M. (2007) *Gifted and Talented in the Early Years Practical Activities for Children Aged 3 to 5.* London: Sage.

Sutherland, R. (2007) *Teaching for Learning Mathematics.* Maidenhead: OUP.

Swan, M. (2001) 'Dealing with misconceptions in mathematics', in P. Gates (ed.), *Issues in Mathematics Teaching.* London: Routledge Farmer.

Thompson, I. (2010) 'Progression in the teaching of multiplication', in I. Thompson (ed.) *Issues in Teaching Numeracy in Primary Schools.* Maidenhead: OUP.

Thompson, I. and Bramald, R. (2002) *An Investigation of the Relationship between Young Children's Understanding of the Concept of Place Value and Their Competence at Mental Addition.* Newcastle upon Tyne: University of Newcastle.

TIMSS (2007) *International Mathematics Report: Findings from IEA's Trends in International Mathematics and Science Study at the Fourth and Eighth Grades.* Available at: http://timss.bc.edu/timss2007/mathreport.html (accessed 28 June 2011).

Treffers, A. and Beishuizen, M. (1999) 'Realistic mathematics education in the Netherlands', in I. Thompson (ed.) *Issues in Teaching Numeracy in Primary Schools.* Buckingham: OUP.

Tucker, K. (2005) *Mathematics Through Play in the Early Years.* London: Paul Chapman Publishing.

Turner, S. and McCullough, J. (2004) *Making Connections in Primary School.* London: David Fulton Ltd.

Twiselton, S. (2000) 'Seeing the wood for the trees: the National Literacy Strategy and Initial Teacher Education; pedagogical content knowledge and the structure of subjects', *Cambridge Journal of Education* 30(3): 393–403.

Van den Heuvel-Panhuizen, M. (1999) 'Context problems and assessment: ideas from the Netherlands', in I. Thompson (ed.) *Issues in Teaching Numeracy in Primary Schools.* Buckingham: OUP.

Von Glasersfeld, E. (1984) 'An introduction to radical constructivism', in P. Watzlawick (ed.) *The Invented Reality.* London: Naughton and Co.

Von Glasersfeld, E. (1995) *Radical Constructivism: A Way of Knowing and Learning.* London: Falmer.

Watson, A. and Mason, J. (1998) *Questions and Prompts for Mathematical Thinking.* Derby: ATM.

Williams, J.S. and Ryan, J. (2007) *Children's Mathematics 4–15: Learning from Errors and Misconceptions.* Maidenhead: Open University Press.

Williams, P. (2008) *Independent Review of Mathematics Teaching in Early Years Settings and Primary Schools.* London: DCSF.

Wilson, S., Shulman, L. and Richert, A. (1987) '150 different ways of knowing: representations of knowledge in teaching', in J. Calderhead (ed.) *Exploring Teachers' Thinking.* London: Cassell, pp. 104–124.

Winter, J., Andrews, J., Greenhough, P., Hughes, M., Salways, L. and Ching Yee, W. (2009) *Improving Primary Mathematics Linking Home and School.* London: Routledge.

World Economic Forum (2011) *The Global Competitiveness Report 2011–2012.* Available at: http://reports.weforum.org/global-competitiveness-2011-2012/ (accessed 9 September 2011).

Wright, T. (2010) *How to be a Brilliant Mentor: Developing Outstanding Teachers.* London: Routledge.

Young-Loveridge, J. (1989) 'The development of children's number concepts: the first year of school', *New Zealand Journal of Educational Studies* 24(1): 47–64.

Zan, R. and Di Martino, P. (2007) 'Attitude toward mathematics: overcoming the positive/ negative dichotomy', *The Montana Mathematics Enthusiast*, Monograph 3: 157–168.

INDEX

Page references in *italics* indicate a figure and those in **bold** show a table.